Type

Time Management

*A timely collection
of stories, ideas, and
suggestions from
people of 16 different
personality types*

Sharon Fitzsimmons, Ph.D.

Canadian Cataloguing in Publication Data

Fitzsimmons, Sharon.
Type and time management

Includes bibliographical references.
ISBN 0-929022-21-1

  1. Time management--Psychological aspects. 2. Myers-Briggs
Type Indicator. I. Psychometrics Canada Ltd. II. Title.
HD69.T54F57 1999   650.1   C99-910676-7

Author: Sharon Fitzsimmons, Ph.D.

Book Design & Composition: Jack Born

MBTI and Myers-Briggs Type Indicator are registered trademarks of
Consulting Psychologists Press, Inc.

Published By:
Psychometrics Canada Ltd.
7125 - 77 Ave.
Edmonton, AB
Canada, T6B 0B5
Tel: (780) 469 2268
Fax: (780) 469 2283
E-mail: info@psychometrics.com
Website: www.psychometrics.com

Printed in Canada

Table of Contents

Acknowledgements

I would like to express my warmest appreciation to the ninety wonderful people of the sixteen different personality types who generously contributed their time, enthusiasm, stories, and ideas to this project. Without their experience and insights, this book would not have been possible.

An extra thank you to those who took the time to read the responses from the other people of their own type, and submitted additional comments, suggestions, and notes of affirmation. Their input was much appreciated and carefully considered for this book.

Thank you also, to the many Myers-Briggs Type Indicator® (MBTI®) enthusiasts who assisted with recruiting people of hard-to-find types. What a warm, friendly, and helpful community of interested people! Their enthusiasm and encouragement helped each time I got to difficult spots and was tempted to give up. I can not acknowledge them by name, because I do not even know all their full names, but I want each of them to know how much ! appreciated their support.

My heartfelt thanks to Donald Macnab, who patiently helped to shape this book and guide the editorial process. Thank you also to Susan Smith and Naomi Quenk who offered their perspectives as experienced authors, and to Danielle Poirier, Shirley Winlaw-Tierney, and Sarah Karl who offered suggestions based on their knowledge and experience with the MBTI. Thank you to the friendly staff at Psychometrics Canada Ltd. who shared the viewpoints of the many people who use the Myers-Briggs Type Indicator. Thank you to Shawn Bakker, Mark Fitzsimmons, Heather Fitzsimmons, and Rod Frey for their editorial assistance, and a special thank you to Jack Born who captured the spirit of the book with his cover and layout design.

My greatest supporter throughout this whole undertaking has been my husband, George Fitzsimmons, who cheerfully lived through each of the seven book drafts, and steadfastly offered his encouragement and enthusiasm. I have him to thank, also, for the inspired idea of recruiting my volunteers through e-mail, and for the countless other ways he made this project possible.

About the Author:

Sharon Fitzsimmons (INFP) is a teacher, author, and qualified MBTI consultant. She received her Ph.D. in Education in 1995, after her children were grown. She has written several textbooks, and is interested in developing workshop curriculum on a variety of topics.

Type & Time Management

Introduction

Introduction

Is time management a thorny issue in your life? Is it something which causes problems and often makes you feel like a failure? Is it something that makes you feel stressed, pressed, overwhelmed, or even angry - with yourself... or with others who try to impose their so-called excellent systems on you?

If you answered 'yes' to any of these questions, this book will be a refreshing change... and it may help you find some practical answers which work for YOU!

We are all unique individuals, so a time management solution which works for one person does not necessarily work for another. But at the same time we share similarities with some people and differences with others. When we do come upon a 'kindred spirit', it's often a great pleasure, and a feeling of "wow! there's somebody else around here who's like me!"

There is a good chance that those 'kindred spirits' share your own personality type, or have a personality similar to yours.

Imagine yourself among a group of people who are more or less like you. You are all sitting around the kitchen table, having a cup of coffee, laughing, talking, and relaxing. Someone mentions a problem and someone else says, "That happens to me too!" Soon you are all telling stories and in the process, you are getting ideas from each other.

Reading parts of this book will be a little like that. You may find a circle of people who are similar to yourself, and you can listen to them sharing stories about their encounters with time management. Some will tell about solutions which worked for them. When you are finished, you will have a few new ideas to try in your own life.

You will also have a chance to 'listen in' on the conversations of people who are different from you. This will help you to better understand those whose time management habits tend to frustrate or annoy you.

This book is for all kinds of people. Many readers will be able to see applications to their own lives and the lives of their friends and family.

For time management coaches, counsellors, and workshop leaders, this book will provide a new way to approach time management issues with different kinds of people. People interested in doing time management counselling or time management workshops will learn about some exciting new research and its applications. Everyone will have a bit of fun sharing stories, ideas, and suggestions.

Why We Need Different Approaches to Time Management

When I first told my friends I was writing a book on time management, they tended to eye me suspiciously. "Why do you want to do that?" they asked. "I hate time management," someone said. "It's just one more thing to feel guilty about."

Of course their doubts were to be expected. Why should I be writing a book about time management? I'm no sterling example of time management efficiency myself, although I do get things done when I need to. I've certainly done my share of forgetting, neglecting, hurrying, worrying, panicking, and apologising... in a variety of situations: teaching, parenting, free lance writing, and volunteer work. Over the years, I've found solutions which work for me. But those ideas won't work for my husband, my son, or my daughter. They each have their own ways of getting things done (or not done, whichever the case may be).

Perhaps not being a time management 'expert' is one reason for writing this book. Maybe we don't always need 'experts' to tell us how to manage our time and run our lives. What we need is a chance to talk about our successes and difficulties with people who understand our personalities and natural preferences. Each of us needs to develop our own time management style which takes our differences into consideration.

Differences From Birth

I first became aware of the need for different approaches to time management when I was an elementary schoolteacher. It seemed that even the youngest children already had their own time management style. Little Jennifer, at seven years old, was already neat and efficient, arranging her pencils and crayons in an orderly way before beginning a task. Sarah, on the other hand, was usually busy chatting with her friends until the last minute, and then she had to hunt for her things before she hurriedly got the job done before running out for recess.

I was young and single at the time, and I blamed the parents for these differences. I assumed that Jennifer must have well organized parents who nurtured her efficient ways. I thought Sarah's parents were free spirits who never bothered to teach her anything.

Then I had children of my own. They both had the same parents and grew up in the same home, yet they were totally different. Even their approaches to homework assignments were different.

My son would plan the whole essay in his head before writing it down: thesis statement first, then supporting ideas and conclusion. My daughter would write down ideas as they came to mind and the essay would just evolve. She cried if anyone insisted that she follow a plan.

Talking with other parents, I discovered that no matter how tidy and methodical the mom or dad, there is no guarantee that the child will turn out that way. It seems that people are just born to approach their work in different ways.

Many years of research into personality differences convince us that this is true. We are all different to varying degrees, so techniques and strategies which work naturally for one person do not work well for another. Yet we can all get things done dependably and often creatively, if only we can find the time management style which suits our own personalities.

Identifying Your Personality Type

This book will help you to use knowledge about your own personality to choose time management strategies which are most comfortable for you. If you have not already done so, you will need to take the Myers-Briggs Type Indicator® (MBTI®) and verify your personality type.

The MBTI is a self-report questionnaire designed to help you to identify your strengths, special gifts, motivations and potential areas for growth. The MBTI is currently the most widely used instrument for understanding normal personality differences and their implications. If you have not had an opportunity to take the Myers-Briggs Type Indicator, you may seek out a qualified practitioner to help you do so. Contacting any of the organizations at the end of the reference section of this book may help you find out how you can take the Myers-Briggs Type Indicator and have it interpreted for you in a clear and ethical way.

Some Background on Personality Type Theory

The concept of personality type is based on a theory developed by Carl Jung (1875-1961) to explain differences in human behaviour. This theory was further studied and applied to human interaction by Katharine Cook Briggs (1875-1968) and her daughter, Isabel Briggs Myers (1897-1980). Their work was the foundation for 50 years of research and development of the current Myers-Briggs Type Indicator.

Personality Type Theory, as it is used today, explains how differences in people's behaviour are caused by the way people prefer to use their minds. According to this theory, there are two major mental activities: taking in information (Perceiving); and organizing information and coming to conclusions (Judging). There are two opposite ways to perceive: Sensing and Intuiting; and there are two opposite ways to judge: Thinking and Feeling. Everyone uses all these processes every day in their external lives (Extraversion) and in their internal lives (Introversion); but we have natural preferences for either using one kind of perceiving or one kind of judging either in our external or in our internal lives. The variations in people's preferences lead to predictable patterns of behaviours. A person's personality type is formed from the predictable patterns of behaviour resulting from their natural preferences.

People with a preference for Judging (J) try to live a planned and organized life, while people with a preference for Perceiving (P) are more comfortable with a spontaneous and flexible lifestyle.

People who prefer Sensing (S) like to perceive information directly through their five senses. They like to focus on the reality around them. People who prefer iNtuiting (N) tend to focus on ideas and possibilities rather than the here-and-now.

People with Thinking preferences (T) like to make decisions by organizing and structuring information and then coming to conclusions in a logical and objective way. People with Feeling preferences (F) like to make their decisions in a more personal, values-oriented way.

People with a preference for Extraversion (E) tend to draw energy from the external world of people, things, and activities. People with a preference for Introversion (I) tend to draw energy from the inner world of reflection, ideas, and impressions.

The combinations of these preferences cause variations in personalities. The Myers-Briggs Type Indicator identifies your preferences and reports your personality type using a four-letter code. There are 16 possible combinations of preferences so there are 16 different personality types.

Characteristics Associated with Each Personality Type

If you have taken the Myers-Briggs Type Indicator, but are not sure you remember your four-letter code, it may help you to read the description of characteristics associated with each type at the beginning of each chapter. These descriptions focus on behaviours and characteristics likely to influence time management. Other descriptions of type can be found in the books listed in the reference section.

Hearing Success Stories

This book is based on the idea that if we hear how people with different kinds of personalities successfully manage their time, we can find out what works for some people and what works for others. If we listen to people who are like ourselves, and learn how they achieve what they do, we might be able to use some of their ideas. If we listen to people unlike ourselves, we begin to understand them better.

My Ph.D. thesis focused on the power of storytelling as a tool for understanding and learning from one another, so I used this approach to encourage people to tell stories about time management. People were asked to tell about times when they were successful and about the kinds of difficulties they often have. They were given opportunities to offer time management suggestions which would be suitable for people with personalities like their own.

Eventually, I collected time management stories, ideas and suggestions from over 80 people of 16 different personality types. There were at least five contributions from people of each personality type. After the stories were collected, they were sent back to people with similar personalities to see if the material seemed useful.

The reactions were extraordinarily affirming. Even the people who had been skeptical about time management said that they found the stories interesting and thought provoking. People of each personality type made remarks like, "This makes sense to me!" "I didn't know there were other people out there who have the same problems as me. Their suggestions are really useful!"

So many people were eager to learn from one another. "This is one time management book I'm looking forward to reading." "At last someone is taking into consideration who I am instead of who I ought to be!" "What a great resource this is going to be!"

I was amazed at the frank way people had told their stories. Many admitted to all kinds of time management difficulties and were able to laugh at themselves. Then they described their own tried and true ways of overcoming their problems.

Some of the solutions suggested by some people sounded bizarre to me at first, but when I shared those ideas with people with similar personalities, the reaction was very positive. Sometimes the ideas that seemed most strange to me were the ones which made the most sense to them! No wonder one time management strategy doesn't work for everyone!

As you read this book, you will learn about the experiences of people like yourself, and of people who are different from you. No matter which personality type you identify with, you should be able to find ideas which suit your own unique preferences and needs. The stories and advice are interesting and entertaining, sometimes painful and often funny. Every individual can find inspiration, encouragement, and practical advice.

Using this Book

Each chapter of this book focuses on one of the 16 MBTI personality types identified by the Myers-Briggs Type Indicator (MBTI). You will probably want to begin by reading the chapter which refers to your own personality type. Later, you may want to read the chapters which refer to the personality types of your family, friends, or co-workers.

In the first section of each chapter, there is a brief description of some of the characteristics and behaviours often observed in people of that personality type. It is not meant to be a comprehensive description; rather, the emphasis is on those characteristics which seem most likely to affect time management.

Following the description, you will find a collection of personal stories and suggestions, as five or more people of each personality type responded to these four questions:

1. *Tell me about an occasion when you felt really successful in managing your time.*
2. *Tell me about some of your difficulties in time management.*
3. *What advice can you offer to others of your type regarding time management?*
4. *What help would you like to get regarding time management?*

The responses are presented exactly as they were given so you can 'hear the voices' of other people who share your preferences. Because there is much variation within each of the 16 identified personality types, some of the stories may resonate with you more than others.

The second section of each chapter contains a discussion of the stories, ideas, and suggestions, and a point form 'guide' to help people of each personality type to 'find their own way.'

The last part of this book provides some ideas for looking more closely at the stories to further explore the link between personality type and time management style. Your attention is drawn to some dramatic contrasts between different personality types. Further questions are also raised, highlighting excerpts from some stories which illustrate why people with different personality types need to find effective time management styles which suit their own preferences. Several issues are touched on: for example, variations in different personality types regarding the need for control or the need to serve others, and how these affect time management style. We also consider how time management choices can enhance or destroy creativity or work satisfaction for certain personality types.

Cautions

Each personality type and each individual has their own strengths and special gifts. No one is 'better' or 'worse' than anyone else. You may use each of the preferences to some degree, so you will find that sometimes you behave like someone of a different type. This is why it might be useful for you to read chapters other than the one which focuses on your type.

Although the MBTI is one of the most valid and reliable self-report personality inventories, you make the final decision about who you really are and what works best for you. Remember also that your personality type does not indicate a measure of your skill or ability in any area; it merely indicates your preference. Many people are capable of performing effectively in non-preferred ways. You will find that several of the participants in this book tell stories of how they found ways to manage time which they did not naturally prefer. The trick was to find ways which were still somewhat palatable, and not totally against their natural inclinations.

Have fun with this book, and hopefully, you will find some useful ideas and suggestions to enhance your own time management style.

Chapter *1*

ENFJ

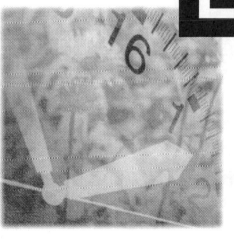

An Introduction to ENFJ

If you are an ENFJ, you are probably friendly and tactful, and work well with people. You carry out your duties in a conscientious and orderly way, persevering until the job is done.

You probably appreciate systems, policies and procedures which enable people to work well together. You understand that a job needs to be done and it is people who do it. You believe in the importance of team effort. Sometimes, in your efforts to contribute to the team effort, you may try to do too much and may feel fragmented or pulled in too many directions. Being responsive to others, your time may be used up trying to meet other people's needs instead of your own.

Your time management problems may stem from your good will to others, which might mean giving a helping hand instead of doing your work. You may be exploited by others who use you and your time to talk over their troubles. But generally, you are able to meet your deadlines, even though you may find yourself a bit frazzled in the process.

Here are how six ENFJs are trying to cope with time management issues. These ENFJs are not necessarily typical of their types, but their stories can provide helpful insights and ideas for you and others. Several identify how they make the most of the strengths which result from their type preferences, and several tell how they compensate for their natural weaknesses. Some tell of difficulties yet unsolved. Together they provide some unique ideas and useful suggestions for ENFJs.

Stories, Ideas, & Suggestions

Doug

Even as I reply I am dealing with an ENFJ's response to time. I have a full day's work ahead of me but I am strongly motivated to reply. First my 'F' says that as a fellow student/learner/human I owe it to you and the others you will share this information with. Second my 'J' says, 'Get it done , then you can focus all of your energy on the task at hand.' That 'J' part also means getting rid of one more piece of paper.

Q. *Tell me about an occasion when you felt really successful in managing your time.*

In 1983 I ran the *National Capital Marathon* in Ottawa, Canada. I had been running for several years but never more than five or six miles at a time. To prepare for the marathon I read several people's plans for success. I chose the one that made sense for me. I planned twelve weeks of preparation and then wrote the plan on a calendar. I ran every day with the mileage planned for each day and each week. I followed the plan without deviation and completed the marathon in three hours twenty-eight minutes. I did the same again in 1987. As I worked through the process I would repeat to myself *'Plan the work. Work the plan.'*

Q. *Tell me about some of your difficulties in time management.*

My difficulties in time management are that I am easily distracted by people issues. If I have to chose between task and people I will do the people process first. However, because of Puritan work ethic, stubbornness, pride, (perhaps those are all labels for the 'J' preference) I will complete the task on time even if it means giving up sleep or recreation time. I use a daytimer and it is important that I plan in advance and check each evening/morning. I can get caught up in the events of the day and forget important responsibilities. The other thing I have learned as a manager who was aware of his people preference that when I was involved in a project and trying not to get off track my 'cold attitude' has hurt and angered others and as an 'F' I can be labelled arrogant or haughty and rude. It is hard for me to stay focused on task so I need to be more gentle with myself and others as I grow into a balanced approach. I need to put down my pencil or leave the computer and avoid the 'N' thing so that I can be 'in the moment' as I continue to learn from my 'S' daughter.

Deb

(An ENFJ who has worked 20 years in an ISTJ culture and learned a lot from it!)

Here are my thoughts and experiences...

A Success in Managing My Time - this was when I was part of a group who had worked hard to establish the mission, our vision, our goals for the cycle, and how we would allocate our human resources in the team. Once I was clear on my role within this group, I was very effective in leading the project, managing my time, and managing the outputs.

Difficulties in Time Management - forcing myself to work on something just because it's in my planner, but I haven't iNtuited it enough inside my head to truly understand the big picture. I used to make myself do it anyway because it was there; now I let my head rule the planner and let the planner be my reminder not my dictator.

Advice to Other ENFJs - You need to know when it is appropriate to realistically estimate the amount of time it will take to accomplish something (it's always longer than you realize); and how to sequence events so that there are fewer surprises in implementation. Involve stakeholders early on and not have to back up later in the project. Dominant feeling will help you to really determine the best choice for the moment, putting people before things, regardless of what the planner says.

Karen

I will try to help, although I need to be brief!

Q. *Tell me about an occasion when you felt really successful in managing your time.*

Recently, I have started giving myself a time frame to complete something, rather than just diving into it and taking as much time as necessary. For example, I frequently write proposals. They take many hours and I could spend three or more hours just fine tuning, continuing to tighten up and improving the formatting. Right before vacation, I needed to complete two proposals. I set two and a half hours as my target for one of the proposals. It actually took three hours, wasn't as polished as I would normally desire, but I got it out to the client and they thought it was great.

Q. *Tell me about some of your difficulties in time management.*

Mostly, I try to accomplish an awful lot every day. I am a business owner, mother of two, homeowner, spouse, child, and sister. It is an awful lot to juggle. Prioritizing and scheduling are the only ways I keep sane.

Q. *What advice can you offer to others of your type regarding time management?*

Although I am an ENFJ, my 'J' preference is not very strong. I can easily pass for a 'P' which affects my time management ability. For ENFJ's - set up your life's mission, review and revise often. Follow Stephen Covey's *First Things First Principles* including setting aside 45 minutes per week to plan your goals for the following week. From these goals (e.g., working out three times per week), schedule the activities necessary to achieve these goals. e.g. Wed. 6:00 p.m. Tennis with Janice. The things you really want to/must do have to be scheduled into your calendar. Otherwise, something or someone will use that time up for you!

Q. *What help would you like to get regarding time management from others of your type?*

How to say 'no' without offending or feeling guilty.

Melinda

Q. Tell me about an occasion when you felt really successful in managing your time.

I think that I am most successful when I have the most to do. One particular week a few years ago, I worked at my full-time job, taught a University class both weekends (Friday evening, all day Saturday, and Sunday afternoon), and we closed on one house, sold the other, and moved. I think I may have even taught another Monday night class. When I am in this kind of situation, I am able to concentrate on just what is the most critical. It helped to have a spouse who had the time and was willing to coordinate the move and no kids to deal with, as they are grown!

Q. Tell me about some of your difficulties in time management.

When I don't have a lot of 'have-to-do's,' I feel like I waste my time on non-important stuff. Also, I think that being intuitive, it is easy for me to get distracted from what I am doing and jump to something else. For instance, I started to answer these questions, had a thought about something that needed to go on my calendar, and while I was at it, did several other things related to my calendar, almost forgetting that I had started this. I also tend to be obsessive about gathering all of the information I can about a subject or project, such as a presentation I will be doing at a conference in a couple of weeks. It is only for an hour and a half, but it is not something I have done much with, so I have spent hours going through potential material to make sure I don't miss any helpful ideas or juicy tidbits. Ironically, the topic is 'Balancing Work and Home!'

Q. What advice can you offer to others of your type regarding time management?

I can give advice that I don't always practice, but what I TRY to do is not be everything to everybody and be willing to say NO. This works about a quarter of the time. Also, chunking down and focusing is helpful—I get too overwhelmed sometimes when I look too far ahead at all I have to do. Schedule regular exercise. I also have to really MAKE myself take time to play..!

Joanne

Successes at managing time:

Most often... I'm very good at looking at 'months-at-a-glance', planning my whole fall, for instance. I'm a consultant and must coordinate my schedule with other consultants and with about seven clients at any given time.

I often get bombarded with last- minute crisis, and I believe I've managed to train my clients into a routine-visit based service to enable me to better plan my days. I'm very successful at gauging traffic time as well. I work in a large city, and often have to drive 45 minutes to an hour between client sites. I'm never late, in spite of traffic and accidents!

Difficulties:

I get very stressed forcing myself to meet my scheduled appointments. For example, if I need to be somewhere for 11:00, and it's a half hour drive, I'll start to worry and hurry at 10:00 - sometimes making people feel like I'm rushing them.

Advice to Other ENFJs:

Keep a routine, and keep your life uncomplicated. I've had to seek advice from a psychologist because I'm borderline 'workaholic' - pushing all the time and bringing closure too quickly.

Q. What help would you like to get regarding time management from others of your type?

I'd like an understanding and respect for 'my' schedule. Others often neglect to observe meeting time deadlines and chat for hours or expect me to drop something and help them. My job is 100% scheduled and others don't seem to respect my schedule.

I'd also like tips on learning to say 'no'! I have a great deal of trouble refusing to help someone, and seem to take on other people's work.

Meg

I am interested in your topic. I teach a time management class for someone who designed the course. She also does a lot of work with Myers-Briggs, as do I. We both think that the course could be much better if designed to the types' needs rather than generic time management principles. I've observed that 'Fs' generally value the prospect of saying no to requests. 'Ps' are not that interested in time management systems but are more interested in procrastination techniques.

I hesitated to respond because time management is not that big of an issue for me. That is both a curse and a gift. My children are both in college this year which means I don't have the demands that kids at home bring. Work has slowed down this year but is picking up dramatically soon. Maybe I would have a different response then.

I don't belong to organizations that demand my time. I spent 2-3 years in New Mexico learning to 'be' rather than 'do'. So I guard my time well. I think time management is more about making choices about what is important, what matches your values, how much money you really need, where your time is best spent.

Q. Tell me about an occasion when you felt really successful in managing your time.

I usually manage my time well. When I have things to do I allow plenty of time to get things done. Time management is not a problem.

Q. Tell me about some of your difficulties in time management.

Difficulties in time management are more about WHAT I am going to do rather than when. I NEED to have something to accomplish, so if that doesn't come my way, I create it. When I have to do something that isn't pleasurable, like designing a handout on a computer, or making a difficult call, or preparing for a course I don't like, I will find other easier, more attractive, shorter things to do. That way I can cross them off my list and feel I have accomplished something.

Another difficulty is that I work out of my home. Home chores can distract me from some of the more unpleasant tasks.

I am grateful when a personal phone call comes through when I am working on the computer. It is a relief from such focused frustrating work. It also is a distraction... that I welcome and don't tend to cut short. Extraverted feeling.

Q. What advice can you offer to others of your type regarding time management?

Check into your own value system to decide where to spend your time. Too often we are driven by the requests and needs of others. Then we can resent that. Learn to speak up and say no. Not everyone's feelings will be hurt by a no. You may have very rational reasons for denying a request at home or at work.

Q. What help would you like to get regarding time management from others of your type?

How do you pull things off that are thrown at you at the last minute? How do you manage your anxiety level?

Discussion

The ENFJ contributors seemed warm and friendly and willing to help. They often mentioned the feelings or opinions of others in their stories.

Although almost all of the ENFJs were able to tell at least one successful time management story, they seemed prone to a common difficulty: saying 'no' to other's requests.

This was not surprising. According to type theory, the force that animates ENFJs is the need to respond to others and get things settled. ENFJs are irresistibly drawn to facilitating, organizing, and making closure while simultaneously meeting others' needs. As my ENFJ friend, Shirley, tells me, "there is often a horrendous conflict with doing what was planned versus being available for people who need your time." Yet, responding to the needs of others is such a driving force for their lives that it would be useless for any time management consultant to advise ENFJs to ignore all the people who are clamouring for their attention. This would be like asking them to avoid life!

The contributors to this study seemed to understand this. When asked to provide suggestions for others like themselves, they offered only ideas which would enable ENFJs to respond to the needs of others, while attending a little more to their own needs as well. They suggested: "Work for balance between the needs of people and demands of the task." "Try not to be everything to everybody." "Try to find a way to get others to understand and respect your schedule." "Learn to speak up and say no... you may have very rational reasons for denying a request at home or at work." "Make yourself take time to play." "Schedule regular exercise." "Check into your own value system to decide where to spend your time. Too often we are driven by the requests and needs of others..."

Since ENFJs are driven to respond to the needs of others and that requires time (you can't hurry when you're dealing with people's needs), they have to be well organized. Perhaps their need for efficiency is even greater than the ESFJs, because their work may lead them into more abstract or theoretical issues which can be more time consuming. Some of the suggestions included: "Set up your life's mission, review and revise often." "Set aside 4-5 minutes per week to plan your goals for the following week. From these goals, schedule the activities necessary to achieve these goals." "Chunk down and focus." "Try to sequence events so there are fewer surprises in implementation." "Involve stakeholders early on so you do not have to back up later in the project."

ENFJs know that no matter how much effort they put into creating a schedule, there are still going to be interruptions and demands from others. They also know that they could not live comfortably with the guilt of not at least considering responding to these requests. So one suggestion was: "Make choices based on your feeling, putting people before things, regardless of what the planner says." Since at least some of the interruptions are going to happen anyway, "expect that it will take longer than you expect to accomplish something."

As mentioned earlier, type should not be an excuse for behaviour. Rather, an understanding of a person's natural preferences can be helpful in the development of an effective style which embraces whatever provides the driving force and gives life its meaning. The contributors offered some useful suggestions to help ENFJs to deal with the conflict between attending to human needs while meeting the demands of the task.

Helping ENFJs Find their Own Way

Characteristics and behaviours which could be expected of an ENFJ

- friendly
- tactful
- work well with people
- conscientious
- orderly
- persevering
- appreciate good team-work

- may try to do too much
- may feel led in too many directions
- responsive to others
- may neglect own needs
- may be exploited by others
- generally able to meet your deadlines

Driving forces
Attending to human needs while facilitating, organizing and making closure.

Problems *most* likely to occur
Conflict between the desire to make closure and the pull to serve human needs.

Solutions *least* likely to be followed
Avoid the people that are clamouring for your attention.

Suggestions

Try these ideas which may help you to complete your work, respond to the needs of others, and attend to your own needs as well.

1. Work for balance between needs of people and demands of the task.

- Try not be everything to everybody.
- Try to find a way to get others to understand and respect your schedule.
- Learn to speak up and say no. Not everyone's feelings will be hurt by a no. You may have very rational reasons for denying a request at home or at work.
- Find out how others say 'no' gently and tactfully.
- Check into your own value system to decide where to spend your time. Too often we are driven by the requests and needs of others. Then we can resent that.
- Schedule regular exercise.
- Make yourself take time to play.
- Keep a routine, and try to keep your life uncomplicated! (if you can!)

2. Improve your organizational skills so that you can more comfortably meet at least some of the demands in your life.

- Set up your life's mission, review and revise often.
- Follow Stephen Covey's *First Things First Principles* including setting aside 4-5 minutes per week to plan your goals for the following week. From these goals, schedule the activities necessary to achieve these goals.
- Chunk down and focus.
- Try to sequence events so there are fewer surprises in implementation.
- Involve stakeholders early on so you do not have to back up later in the project.

3. Know that the unexpected is bound to occur.

- Expect that it will take longer than you expect to accomplish something.
- Make choices based on your feeling, putting people before things, regardless of what the planner says.

4. Consider alternatives.

If you think you might be becoming a workaholic, seek the advice of a professional (e.g. psychologist).

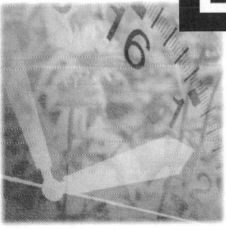

Chapter 2

ENFP

An Introduction to ENFP

If you are an ENFP, you are likely to be energetic, creative and full of original ideas. You value inspiration and work enthusiastically if the task kindles your interest and seems meaningful to you. You dislike routine, preferring variety and 'spur of the moment' activities, often involving other people.

Orderly and predictable systems probably seem stifling to you. On the other hand, in the absence of structure, you may want to do so many different things at once that you may end up being pulled in too many directions. Fortunately, doing many things at once actually has an energizing effect on you, which may enable you to pull through at the last minute.

In your enthusiasm to be involved in so many things and with so many people, you may have difficulty knowing your own physical, time, and mental limits. You may become overextended or distracted from completing the tasks you have started.

With your contagious enthusiasm, multitude of ideas, and ability to motivate and inspire people, you have the potential to accomplish many things. The problem is to find ways to follow through and complete the task without losing interest or getting distracted.

Here are how seven ENFPs are trying to cope with time management issues. These ENFPs are not necessarily typical of their types, but their stories can provide helpful insights and ideas for you and for others. Several identify how they capitalize on the strengths which result from their type preferences, and several tell how they compensate for their natural weaknesses. Some tell of great frustrations and problems yet unsolved. Together they provide some unique ideas and useful suggestions for ENFPs.

Stories, Ideas, & Suggestions

Kathy

Greetings... and nice to get correspondence! sorry for the delay in response... have been out of town and away from my beloved computer. Sounds like you have opted for some interesting research and I would be happy to participate. (Maybe I will figure some things out here along the way!) And yes, would be interested in seeing your results... what will you be using the research for? In conjunction with a column - writing - education...? Whatever... I know that sometimes things are not clear in the beginning of an idea and when there is response and such, an energy builds and more possibilities and imaginings come forth... so for what it's worth, I hope this compilation of yours serves your highest good and needs. (and thank you for allowing me to answer the questions... as TIME MANAGEMENT has been one of my challenges lately!) Interesting, how the Universe works things into my space! Get prepared for the following responses to probably skew the typical results... I promise to be honest and vulnerable.

Q. *Tell me about an occasion when you felt really successful in managing your time.*

This is the easiest to answer... right now, anyway! I am in the midst of coordinating workshops and seminars across the country for my associate, who has just published a book. Because there are specific deadlines to be met, I find that I am extraordinarily efficient in completing phone calls and paperwork. I am able to really plan out my hours in the day, realizing that there is only a finite amount of time with which I can work, and VERY SPECIFIC GOALS that I want to achieve. Which means, I KNOW I must get up at 5:45 a.m. to run, I MUST spend an hour updating my call lists and folders, I MUST be efficient when dropping off the dry cleaning and picking up the food for dinner. I CANNOT spend an hour gabbing on the phone and catching up with people who think I have moved to Mars and making sure that THEY are doing o.k. Not lately, anyway. (Does that make sense?)

Q. *Tell me about some of your difficulties in time management.*

Hmmm... unfortunately, this, TOO, is easy to answer right now. Although I love and long for the 'unrestricted' times, when I can just kind-a lay back and let things proceed at their own pace (pretending that I am being spontaneous and fostering 'creative' time) I find that if I do NOT have specific targets and goals, if I have too much 'time' that is unrestricted, I ruminate, disseminate, compilate, (scream), ponder, make lists, change the lists, (sit in the bathtub, clean the kitchen, do the laundry) make more lists... get caught up in PLANNING instead of DOING (the ugly but true side of the ENFP mind, which loves the dreaming and creative stage and rebels a bit at the necessary but important 'doing the little things' mundane and tedious stage). Lots of 'free spirit' energy runs through my veins - captivating to many people but crazy making when I am forced to finish a project which has lost its thrill. Definitely, without outside stimulation and responsibility and accountability, I can very easily get sidetracked and disinterested. (Eek - what an observation!)

Q. *What advice can you offer to others of your type regarding time management?*

Hmmm... this is kind-a tough, because I know only what works for me. There ARE some days that are 'unscheduled'... as in, no appointments, no speaking engagements, no classes to run... but I know, that for myself, left to my own devices and choices, I would read a book for five hours straight and practice some kind of escapism. What I have come to appreciate over the past couple of years is that it is o.k. sometimes to just tune out and do whatever it is that I think engages me. I have been known to take on a reupholster project in the blink of an eye, or paint the bathroom in a day. Just because I 'see possibilities' and like to act on them with some creative force. I have determined that SOMETIMES, it is o.k. to just 'go with the flow' of whatever is tickling my fancy... I have given myself permission to engage the Muse and not demand measurable (profitable $$$) results from things all the time. In the same breath, I must add that I know SOMETIMES I must discern what exactly I am trying to achieve... and I measure out my activities accordingly. Maybe what I am trying to say is that I keep a visual calendar and 'wish list map' in front of me at all times... to help me remember where I am going and what I am attempting to do. And then I figure out how to prioritize the time accordingly. And I must ALWAYS have new projects to look forward to.

Q. *What help would you like to get regarding time management from others of your type?*

Haha... well, for one, hopefully, that SOME of my propensities are shared by others and do not qualify me for some crazy definition! Honestly, knowing that I am not the only one who seems to not manage 'unrestricted' time well would be a help. But additionally, hearing about other techniques that ENFP's employ to keep them on track and consistent would be great. The visual calendar and my 'treasure map' of goals and wishes USUALLY helps... but it seems like there might be other ways to help me feel like I am progressing and using my time to its best advantage, even when I am in the midst of the 'humdrum' but necessary stuff that needs to be accomplished.

I would love to hear some other responses...

DOES ANY OF THIS HELP? hope so... thanks for the exercise in revealing myself... and good luck with your research!

Peg

I'd love to chat... but I don't have time now! I'm an ENFP and with my tendency to make people happy, and to put things off till I'm 'inspired' I can often get caught in a jam. I'm in one now, so I'll try and respond later.

After a few weeks and a gentle reminder...

Q. *Tell me about an occasion when you felt really successful in managing your time.*

I often feel 'really successful in managing time.' It's the people around me who may feel pressed. I thrive on the last minute crunch that may look like we'll never make it... and then, lo and behold, the project comes through. It may finish at midnight, but it meets customer time-lines, and exceeds expectations.

Q. Tell me about some of your difficulties in time management.

See above. Because I'm a strong 'P', (funny that it's my initial as well) and a strong 'N', I rely on my instincts and last minute 'a-ha' moments to get me through to conclusion on a project. With my experience of coming up with what I need in time (albeit JUST in time), I continue to expect success. And it usually comes.

Q. What advice can you offer to others of your type regarding time management?

Not to be afraid of what may seem like indecision as you gather insights and inspiration. That's just the way we work. On the other hand, knowing that we may get close to the end with yet a lot to do, it's important to clear that working space near deadline... we'll need it.

I think it helps to have a very organized assistant... otherwise, I'm content to be who I am.

Hope this helps... (I'm an ENFP, after all, and I'm here to help!)

Susan

A few thoughts on time...

I am defining time management as effectively using my time to complete work tasks.

Q. Tell me about an occasion when you felt really successful in managing your time.

It seems that I am most successful with my time management when I have multiple intriguing projects going at one time. The requirement to complete all the work on time - coupled with the excitement I have for the projects - allow me to focus on my work and organize tasks.

Q. Tell me about some of your difficulties in time management.

At times, it is very difficult for me to complete even the simplest of tasks. Basically, the task does not completely hold my attention - and I am off doing something else prior to completing the first task. So jumping from one thing to another makes it difficult to finish a task. Therefore, as the day ends, much time is spent - but not much is accomplished (or completed).

Q. What advice can you offer to others of your type regarding time management?

What is most helpful to me in managing time is writing a 'to do' list at the end of the previous day. This list allows me to collect my thoughts, focus on next steps, and provides me a starting point each morning - other than the 'what shall I do now' question I sometimes face each day. Of course, another problem is taking the time to make this list each day. (I need to be more diligent on that.)

Q. What help would you like to get regarding time management from others of your type?

I am always anxious to learn new and better ways to manage my time and be more productive. Techniques on managing time during the completion of routine tasks would be appreciated. I abhor routine tasks - so therefore time management becomes a real concern for me in this case.

Hope this helps. If you have any questions feel free to ask.

Ian

Hope the following is useful to you.

Q. Tell me about an occasion when you felt really successful in managing your time.

When I had a job which functioned on a cyclical basis, it required attention to meeting established time frames. The time frames were regular ones each year, such as a salary and benefits survey being completed by April 30th. This job allowed me leeway with the work itself, as long as each deadline date was met. Secondly, it helped that I understood very well how my work component fitted within the bigger picture, such as the organization's planning or budgeting needs.

Q. *Tell me about some of your difficulties in time management.*

I have tended not to manage time well where there is less structure in the job or the work. The structure provides a framework in which to function 'organizationally' in a more effective manner (for me). With too little structure I find it hard managing my time. I am prone to diversions, distractions and putting things off to the last minute. Sometimes this has added undue pressure at the eleventh hour, where I have left too little time to complete the project or work. A typical distraction for me would be where someone's need seems greater than the completion of the work. I am more likely to attend to what the individual needs first, rather than focus on the task deadline. This has caused me to miss many a deadline. The pay off has usually been the value to the individual who required the help and my satisfaction in being there for someone else.

Q. *What advice can you offer to others of your type regarding time management?*

If you have a deadline to work against make sure you at least look at how much finite time it is likely to take and then plan accordingly, even if that includes some eleventh hour energy burst. It is helpful to commit to the deadline or the project, so that others are not left doubting that we will complete it. I like to know: What do you expect of me? What is the time frame? What kind of leeway do I have? Then if that is agreeable I will work to meet the objectives. With major projects I also prefer to function as a team so that we can be supportive of each other's success.

Q. *What help would you like to get regarding time management?*

I would also like to know if there are others of my type who handle deadlines and distractions better than I do and ask them to help me.

Additional comments... as a right brain person I find some of the organizing tips for the right brainers extremely valuable. I don't feel that this approach invalidates me and in fact supports getting things accomplished. I think this is an important ingredient in a world where most organizing skills and organization itself tends to be left brain based. We need to find more ways to tap into using both sides and honour the differences.

Bonita

Successes at managing time:

Recently I was working full time on a project team and had also agreed to assist another manager in making her employee meetings more fun. I was given more responsibilities for the meeting than I had agreed to and tried to do both things well. When I realized I couldn't do the quality of work I'd like on both, I told the manager I was assisting that I had to concentrate on the project. By choosing where I wanted to concentrate my energies, I could do a complete and thorough job on the project team.

Difficulties at managing time:

I don't plan enough time for tasks. I've learned it will take longer than I think it will. No matter what 'it' is. I often try to do more than one thing at a time. I have a tendency to double book myself. I have difficulty sticking to a schedule and finishing.

Advice to Other ENFPs:

(Why? They don't listen. Hee-hee) Make a list. Do the stuff you don't want to do first. Don't say you'll attend until you check your calendar. Write it down as soon as you say yes. Plan more time than you think you'll need. Complete the task you're working on before you allow yourself to be distracted by something that appears to be more interesting. Get someone who likes to finish things to work with you.

Leslie

Q. Tell me about an occasion when you felt really successful in managing your time.

I'm still waiting to feel successful managing my time. I'm most successful when I'm enjoying what I'm doing. I'm easily distracted when I don't enjoy what I'm doing. I've also found that using computers helps make things more fun. I tend to get it all done but it's often at the last minute with more stress than I would like.

Q. *Tell me about some of your difficulties in time management.*

Distractions, not having the discipline to do my 'Daily Prioritized Task List', not wanting to do what I have to do because I'd rather do what I want to do.

Q. *What advice can you offer to others of your type regarding time management?*

Try to make it fun. Give yourself breaks and rewards for doing things you don't want to do. Set deadlines or better yet get someone else to set a deadline so you'll really meet it.

Q. *What help would you like to get regarding time management from others of your type?*

Any ideas that work would be great. Is there some way to involve others - everything is more fun with others and I'm more motivated to do for others than to do for myself. How can you use a system and not feel stifled by it?

I'd love to hear more about what others say.

Robert

Successes and difficulties at managing time:

I will say that I have always managed my time pretty well, according to markers such as being on time and having my assignments done on time. My style is, now, to prepare ahead, or at least to think about a project well before it is due and let it simmer. Then, when it is actually nearing the due date, I tend to do what is necessary in a fairly quick burst of activity. In other ways I might be seen as wasting time by some, because I have a strong play philosophy and work without balance loses its meaning for me. To fill my calendar full and leave no time to decompress and just be, is anathema. I relish those days when there is nothing on my schedule. I play golf a lot and am able to get outside and step outside of time to some degree. 3-4 hours on a golf course allows me to put time in its proper perspective; it is relative after all, is it not? This allows me to approach work with a fresh sense of enthusiasm.

Advice for ENFPs:

As advice to others, I would say that if you are in a position where work rules your life, you are out of balance and there is a price to pay for that. If you are young, you can postpone some of the tuition, but most likely relationships will suffer. As you get older an imbalance of work can lead to depression and a spiritual deadening. I feel that this imbalance leads us down paths of unnecessary suffering. If your work requires too much of you, you're doing the wrong things. Take time to look up from your work and begin to consider alternatives. Find some help, someone to talk to who can help you take a larger view of work and it's role in your life. Freud said, 'There is work and there is love in a happy life. Working too much will damage the love we have for ourselves and for others. In return we find ourselves increasingly isolated and lonely, diminished of spirit.' Remember, we are human BEINGS, not human DOINGS.

Discussion

As might be expected, the ENFP responses were full of enthusiasm. There was a spirit of fun that effused from many of the ENFP contributors.

Almost all of the ENFP contributors were able to tell at least one time management success story. But almost all seemed prone to a common difficulty: getting distracted or starting new things before the current one is finished.

This was not surprising. According to type theory, the force that animates ENFPs is an intuitive vision of possibilities. ENFPs are irresistibly drawn to new ideas, and find themselves continually plunging into new projects, often involving other people. Since ENFPs are so often dynamic, affirming, and highly skilled with people, they are able to sweep others up in their excitement.

Since the variety and excitement of a never-ending array of new ideas and possibilities is what gives joy to their lives, it would be heartless for any time management consultant to advise ENFPs to improve their 'time management' by asking them to avoid or ignore distractions. This would be like asking them to avoid life!

The contributors to this study seemed to understand this. When asked to provide suggestions for others like themselves, they offered only ideas which would enable ENFPs to enjoy life in their own way, while coping with the demands of the world around them.

Since they know the distractions are not going to go away (Thank goodness, since new ideas and possibilities are the driving force of their lives!), the best thing to do is to work around them:

e.g. "Plan more time than you think you'll need."

Since new possibilities and ideas are always around, you simply have to keep on track in spite of them. e.g. "Keep a visual calendar and a 'wish list map' in front of you... to help remember where you are going..."

ENFPs want life and work to be exciting and enjoyable. The contributors - knowing how essential this is - made such suggestions as "try to make work fun", and "always have new projects to look forward to". Since fun, for them, usually involves other people, they also say: "involve others if possible; work is always more fun with others," and "work as a team if you can, so you can be supportive of each other's successes."

The ENFP contributors did not offer many ideas for detailed planning, because sticking to a schedule does not accommodate the exciting possibilities or surges of creativity that their own work style can offer. Remember when Peg said: "I thrive on the last minute crunch... I depend on my instincts and the last minute "a-ha" moments and when the project comes through, it meets customer time-lines and exceeds expectations."

Some of the contributors did say, however, that they work best if there is some sort of structure in place when they get started. Ian said that, for him, "the structure provides a framework in which to function..." Presumably, this structure had been set up by someone else, and still allowed for flexibility. In addition, there were a few practical suggestions to help ENFPs to avoid getting into a bind. These people know their own vulnerabilities! e.g. "Don't promise until you check your calendar!" "Write it down as soon as you say yes;" "Clarify such things as what is expected of me, what is the time frame, how much leeway do I have;" "Clear the working place near deadline, you're going to need it!" "Try to get an organized assistant;" "Try to get someone who likes to finish things to help you."

While considering all of these suggestions, it is important to note that some of the contributors said they are comfortable with their workstyle just the way it is. Clearly, they had found their own time management style, and do not wish to change it.

"I often feel really successful in managing time, it's the people around me who may feel pressed..."-Peg

"... I might be seen as wasting time by some, because I have a strong play philosophy and work without balance loses its meaning for me. To fill my calendar full and leave no time to decompress and just be, is anathema..."-Robert

"Advice to ENFPs? Why? They won't listen. Hee hee." -Bonita

As mentioned earlier, type should not be an excuse for behaviour. Rather, an understanding of a person's natural preferences can be helpful in the development of an effective style which embraces whatever provides the driving force and gives life its joy and meaning. The contributors offered some useful suggestions to help ENFPs to be more effective time managers while still being themselves.

Helping ENFPs Find their Own Way

Characteristics and behaviours which could be expected of an ENFP

- energetic
- creative
- full of original ideas
- value inspiration
- work enthusiastically if the task seems interesting and meaningful
- dislike routine
- like variety
- enjoy 'spur of the moment' activities involving other people
- can motivate and inspire others
- find predictable systems stifling
- may want to do many different things at once
- often able to pull through at the last minute.
- have difficulty knowing your own limits
- may become overextended

Driving forces
Launching new ideas and possibilities, often involving other people.

Problems *most* likely to occur
Getting distracted.

Solution *least* likely to be followed
Steadfastly work until the job is done.

Suggestions

Here are some suggestions to help you enjoy life in your own way while coping with the demands of the world around you.

1. Expect that there are going to be distractions and diversions.

- Expect that it will take longer than you expect to accomplish something.
- Work for balance between needs of people and demands of the task.
- Keep a visual calendar and a 'wish list map' in front of you at all times to help remember where you are going and what you are attempting to do. Then try to figure out how to prioritize the time accordingly.

2. Keep work and life as fun and exciting as possible.

- Involve others if possible; work is always more fun with others, and that can be a good motivator for getting the job done.
- Always have new projects to look forward to.

3. Try to create a structure with flexibility within it.

- When planning a project, make sure you at least look at how much finite time it is likely to take, even if that includes some eleventh hour energy burst.
- Clarify such things as: what is expected of me? what is the time frame? what kind of leeway do I have?

- Set deadlines, or better yet, get someone else to set a deadline so you'll really meet it.
- Don't promise until you check your calendar! Write it down as soon as you say 'yes'.
- Use a 'pacer' to help to handle deadlines and distractions and keep you on track.

4. Know your own workstyle.

- Don't be afraid of what may seem like indecision as you gather insights and inspiration
- Clear that working place near deadline... you're going to need it!
- Try to get an organized assistant or someone who likes to finish things to work for you.
- Give yourself rewards for doing things you don't like.
- Try to write a 'to do list' at the end of the previous day. This may allow you to collect your thoughts, focus on next steps and provide a starting point for the next morning.
- Look for organizational tips for right brainers.

5. Consider alternatives.

- If you are in a position where work rules your life, you are out of balance. Find someone to talk to who can help you take a larger view of work and its role in your life.

Chapter 3

ENTJ

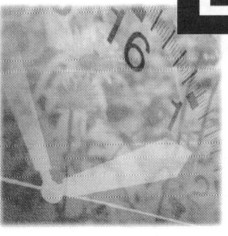

An Introduction to ENTJ

If you are an ENTJ, you are decisive, logical, and strong in reasoning power. You typically take charge and command with assurance. You are quick at acting on problems and finding solutions.

You enjoy leading an organization or group to superior performance, but you are less interested in day-to-day operations. You prefer to manage by making strategic arrangements, leaving the routines and specifics to others.

Your strengths include your ability to marshal forces to achieve future goals. Weaknesses can arise from your lack of attention to details in planning and specific processes in day-to-day operations.

Since you are inclined to manage, it is logical that you should be comfortable at time management too. However, even you can run into time management problems. You can find yourself with sudden surprises, too many problems to solve, and too much to do in the day.

Here are how seven ENTJs are trying to cope with time management issues. These ENTJs are not necessarily typical of their types, but their stories can provide helpful insights and ideas for you and others. Several identify how they make the most of the strengths which result from their type preferences, and several tell how they compensate for their natural weaknesses. Some tell of difficulties yet unsolved. Together they provide some unique ideas and useful suggestions for ENTJs.

Stories, Ideas, & Suggestions

Gayla

Here are my responses - I apologize for the delay (so much for time management!).

Q. *Tell me about an occasion when you felt really successful in managing your time.*

I am usually the most successful when I have a number of projects in the works. Generally, during the third week of the month I have three seminars in three different areas of my state, plus a masters level course I teach at a local University, plus other administrative tasks related to my business. I feel especially successful when I have everything prepared the week before, including handouts, materials and visual aids. Then, as each day begins, I simply review the materials for that day to refresh my memory and 'get my head into the subject matter.'

Q. *Tell me about some of your difficulties in time management.*

My greatest difficulties are usually the result of my over-committing or not anticipating the actual time needed for a project. I love new projects and planning, but sometimes the implementation phase bogs me down. I am, at times, overly optimistic about how much I can get done, and then I get very frustrated when I lag behind or miss deadlines. It drives me nuts to be late on a deadline, and frankly, I get embarrassed about it. (Is this classic ENTJ behaviour, or what?)

Q. *What advice can you offer to others of your type regarding time management?*

First of all, do what I say, not what I do! Seriously, I have a few suggestions:

    a. When planning a project, rely on past experiences to anticipate the time needed. I have learned to keep more detailed notes as I work on projects, which helps me plan the time needed for future projects that are similar in nature. Keeping details, especially after the fact, is a challenge for ENTJ preferences.

b. Don't beat yourself up if you miss a deadline - obviously, other people with differing types don't get so hung up on time and deadlines and will generally understand if you need to negotiate some more time. I do think it's important to let a client, manager, colleague, etc. know in advance when you need more time, and negotiate it with their agreement.

c. Most importantly, take time for yourself. Most ENTJs prefer to get our work done before we play, especially when influenced by a strong "work ethic" environment. I am gradually learning to put work aside to play, which is a challenge for my type as well as my profession as a small business owner.

I hope this is helpful for your research. I am interested in seeing your results.

Jerrold

Q. *Tell me about an occasion when you felt really successful in managing your time.*

Frankly, I have rarely had problems with time management. For the past several years I have been a Covey Leadership Centre Facilitator for *'Seven Habits of Highly Effective People,' 'First Things First,'* and *'Principle Centered Leadership.'* Although I am not a Covey devotee, I have found that his suggestion that time management is not as effective as life leadership is true. Having a clear life purpose (mission) with prioritized roles and goals, makes 'time management' pretty simple, and that's coming from one who is, now, 25 years and some months active duty Air Force, have my own consulting business, and is a full time student in a Masters program in Organizational Leadership.

A specific occasion:

1) Purpose of the project -- planning, organizing, coordinating, and facilitating a strategic planning off-site for the senior executives of a 10,000 member federal organization.

2) Role -- I was the lead for building the agenda, the participant materials and approach to an initial attempt to create a coherent mission, vision, and

values set for the organization. I gathered trusted, competent team members to help create the agenda and approach, and I facilitated the off-site.

3) Initiatives -- I attempted to get xSTJ leaders to look beyond the present and see our organizational possibilities using models from best in class and world class organizations, and to explore some mental imaging.

4) Why it worked out -- The goal was specific. I didn't do it by myself. I know my limits. One important player was someone I would eventually work closely with in many team building activities, an ISFP -- my type opposite. She was magic in helping me see what I could not during preparation.

Q. *Tell me about some of your difficulties in time management.*

A lack of clear focus, goal, or specific desired outcomes create the greatest difficulty. It is hard to begin when you don't know what the end in mind is.

It is not uncommon to have managers and leaders who know what they want in a general sort of way and expect you to find out what that is specifically. What inevitably happens is that the end product isn't what they wanted so they send you back to try again, without any clearer direction. 'I'll know when it's right when I see it' but they can't describe what that is. Doomed to failure, or at a minimum massive frustration.

Q. *What advice can you offer to others of your type regarding time management?*

Have a clear life purpose (mission) with prioritized roles and goals. This advice would not be to just my type, because type should not be an excuse for behaviour. I would recommend this approach to everyone, although I know that not everyone would appreciate it.

M.E.

I hardly ever think about time management -- I'm too busy. I will save your note and try to answer when I get a chance!

Later M.E. wrote:

What an interesting project! I was frazzled when I first got your note. Time management is not a topic I'm very good with. Probably my type -- ENTJ. Or just me -- I'm very interested in your results and hope you will share them.

I usually feel very successful managing time when I have a lot of things happening at once and keep them all going. There have been unfortunate times when I've gone to extremes, gotten over-committed and have felt that I wasn't doing a good job of anything.

I don't have advice for other ENTJs; I'm hoping they'll have some for me. I usually manage all of my activities by never putting anything away. Piles are growing all over my house and office. The minute I try to organize the stuff, I can't find anything.

This isn't much, but it's a start. Thanks for keeping me informed of your progress!

Mary Ellen

Q. *Tell me about an occasion when you felt really successful in managing your time.*

I can't think of specifics, but I can tell you that I always feel successful when I have a list, and then get great joy checking the items off when completed. I have been known to add to the list any items that I accomplished that were not originally on the list. Is this mind games or what? Because, I end up trashing the list! When I just roll with it, I never know what I really have done. There is always this despair that comes over me because I don't recognize all that I have gotten accomplished.

Q. Tell me about some of your difficulties in time management.

Slowing down, trying to do too much in too short of time. I am slowing down and taking time to smell the roses, I just wish I was smarter earlier in life.

Q. What advice can you offer to others of your type regarding time management?

Living in the moment is the number one challenge that I have experienced as an ENTJ. I have always lived for tomorrow and not today. My mind races ahead light years while others around me are in the present. This is the gift and challenge of our type. Hope this helps. I would be interested in your results.

Marvin

Q. Tell me about an occasion when you felt really successful in managing your time.

Each summer I must plan course work for the following University Term. Usually in April the decisions are finalized on selecting a textbook and other supporting materials. By June, the course outline needs to be written. This tells the students what to expect: Content, Assignments, Examinations, Class presentations. etc. I like to use a calendar and specify readings, guest speakers, and curriculum content. This way, I do not have to think about the course all the time. Once the schedule is set, it rules my time with the class, barring special opportunities or more interest than anticipated in a topic. The students receive this course calendar on the first day of classes. It is a kind of contract between us as to what I will provide and what will be expected of them. No debate here. It gives me a sense of control. I know where I am going and so do those most directly affected.

Q. Tell me about some of your difficulties in time management.

Every day is a struggle of personal discipline between the temptations of what else to learn about or try one's hand at; and the necessities of delivering according to the expectations of myself and my job definition. Usually the gainful employment demands win out. When they do not, there is a little guilt while enjoying the 'sinful' deviation of self indulgence.

Q. What advice can you offer to others of your type regarding time management?

Without a daytimer I would be lost. It is necessary to block out time for all major assignments for teaching, writing, concerts, birthdays, etc. Then that time is sacrosanct. It will not be traded or violated because 'first come, first served' and I have committed myself to that block for the specific purpose. A second guideline is to plan far enough ahead, in enough detail, that you can put the project or task on the shelf, at the ready for roll out. Then forget about it and concentrate your energies upon the next priority of the day or week. Third, always ask, "Who else could get this project done instead of me?" If there is any way to hand off, partner, or delegate the task do so. Perhaps you can trust the other to do 90% of the work, you can fine tune it and give them the credit. Second author is better than having to do it all yourself for the honour of first author. After all, accomplishing the task is the goal, not who did it.

Don

Q. Tell me about an occasion when you felt really successful in managing your time.

Getting grades in on time! If you are in academia you understand. At the end of the term we are required to give and mark exams. I usually receive papers as well, then I have to tabulate final grades for the course. This usually takes place in a short period of time because everything is due in the registrar's office the Monday following exams. One specific instance I recall is completing a stack of short (five page) papers from about 50 students in a very short period of time. It was disciplining myself to read them quickly and carefully. But I succeeded. I also use a 'to do' list, which guides me through a day. But it would be easier to tell you of my frustrations at not being able to have success in managing time. I fail more than I succeed.

Q. Tell me about some of your difficulties in time management.

Not working efficiently. Over the years I have developed a set of WATs (work avoidance techniques) and I am quite successful at using them to not get work done. The greatest difficulty I have is not having the mental discipline to focus exclusively on a task for a long period of time usually because there are other things on my plate clamouring for attention. And the tasks are often demanding of hours of work, not minutes (so the stack of papers to grade are sitting on the desk next to this machine but I have only one hour between classes, not what I consider sufficient time to dig into them).

Q. *What advice can you offer to others of your type regarding time management?*

Not sure this is helpful, given my track record. I try to 'psych' myself up to the task. I try to put myself in a mental mode that says 'you will focus on this exclusively for a period of x hours' a day before I do it, then follow it up and reinforce the challenge when I get up in the morning. Trying to find the mental discipline of exclusive concentration on one and only one project at a time.

Linda

Here are my brief responses:

Q. *Tell me about an occasion when you felt really successful in managing your time.*

Almost daily when I review my core values and long-term goals and then select or deselect events for the day, week, month and then assign a sequence to them. What is really cool is to say NO to stuff and actually have some unstructured time left over for, gasp, spontaneity!

Q. *Tell me about some of your difficulties in time management.*

I tend to underestimate how long things will take and I tend to forget to allow for roadblocks caused by things and people over which I have no control. Another difficulty is when someone else makes a mistake and I am stuck with the time-consuming chore of getting it fixed. Such as a mistake on my records somewhere, like a credit card billing or phone bill. It takes hours and days of repetitious phone calls, sometimes even letter writing, to get it fixed. I cannot delete this type of task from my list because, even though they caused the problem or mistake, I am stuck with the consequences of it unless I go and persist in getting it fixed.

Q. *What advice can you offer to others of your type regarding time management?*

Take the Franklin Quest* eight hour class and purchase the planning tool. Use it as taught carefully and intentionally for ninety days. Your life will change, IF you use the whole approach -- particularly the values part as the driver for event selection and deselection.

* nowFranklinCovey

Discussion

As might be expected, the ENTJ contributors were hard to recruit at first, as most of them were so busy. But once I received their stories and ideas, I was struck by two things: the seriousness with which many of them approach their mission to get things accomplished, and the ability of some of them to poke fun at their own efforts. While there were similarities in this group, there was certainly diversity as well.

Almost all of the ENTJ contributors were able to tell at least one time management success story. But they seemed prone to a common difficulty: getting overextended and overworked.

This was not surprising. According to type theory, the force that animates ENTJs is the drive to run as much of the world as may be theirs to run. ENTJs are irresistibly drawn to making decisions, then energizing and directing others to make it happen.

Since the challenge and excitement of a never-ending continuum of new accomplishments and new conquests is what gives purpose to their lives, it would be heartless for any time management consultant to advise ENTJs to avoid getting overextended by not doing so much. This would be like asking them to avoid life!

The contributors to this study seemed to understand this. When asked to provide suggestions for others like themselves, they offered only ideas which would enable ENTJs to control their time in their own way, while attending a little more to their own needs and the requirements of their current objectives.

Since they know all this energy is not going to go away (thank goodness, since it is the driving force of their lives!), the best thing to do is make sure the energy is channelled in well-thought-out directions.

e.g. "Think about Covey's suggestion that time management is not as effective as life leadership. It is important to have a clear life purpose (mission) with prioritized roles and goals."

Since ENTJs like to focus on future objectives, but have little interest in the details essential for implementation or maintenance, many of the suggestions had to do with enlisting others to help with the detail work. "Always ask, 'Who else could get this project done instead of me?' If there is any way to hand off, partner, or delegate the task, do so..." For those ENTJs who can not yet hire someone else to do the detail work, there was encouragement to at least keep aware of the time that would be required for these tasks. "Rely on past experiences to anticipate the time needed for new projects." "Plan far enough ahead, in enough detail, that you can put the project or task on the shelf at the ready for roll out. Then forget about it and concentrate your energies upon the next priority..."

ENTJs want to feel in control (as Jerrold later clarified, not necessarily of others, but of themselves and the situation). This is the only way they can feel comfortable. To attain a sense of control, it is necessary to be well organized. ENTJs were encouraged to: "Take the [FranklinCovey] eight-hour class and buy a planner." "Use a daytimer to block out time for all major assignments..." "When you delegate important tasks to others, make sure your goals are specific (a partner of a different type may be needed to help you identify specific goals and steps needed...)"

None of these ENTJ contributors made suggestions regarding efficient organization of workspace. However, one did say, "I usually manage all of my activities by never putting anything away. Piles are growing all over my house and office. The minute I try to organize the stuff, I can't find anything." I do not know if this is typical of the way ENTJs organize their space but I do know that my ENTJ husband also organizes his office by strata. It is interesting to compare this description with one I received from an ESTJ and see what a difference the sensing auxiliary could make: "I manage to place/store whatever I'm working with the minute I'm finished using it... my files are always up to date and stored at the right place..." My husband gets many things done in spite of the accumulations on his workspace, so perhaps this aspect of organization is not as important to the ENTJ's achievement style as to the ESTJ's.

The ENTJs know they overwork and overextend themselves. That is why they also cautioned each other: "Try hard to live in the present some of the time. Take a few minutes to smell the roses before you're old." "Take time off for yourself, even though your natural preference is to get work done before play." The ENTJs need to be reminded to enjoy the moment and to actually structure recreational activity into their plans. This is certainly true of my ENTJ husband too!

As mentioned earlier, type should not be an excuse for behaviour. Rather, an understanding of a person's natural preferences can be helpful in the development of an effective style which embraces whatever provides the driving force and gives life its meaning. The contributors offered some useful suggestions to help ENTJs to get things accomplished without overextending themselves.

Characteristics and behaviours which could be expected of an ENTJ

- decisive

- logical

- strong in reasoning power

- self-confident

- quick at acting on problems and finding solutions

- enjoys leading an organization or group

- likes to take charge

- can get overextended

- not much interested in day-to-day operations

- can have too much to do in the day

Driving forces

To make decisions that lead to a never-ending continuum of new accomplishments and conquests.

Problems *most* likely to occur

Getting overworked.

Solutions *least* likely to be followed

Avoid getting overextended by not doing so much.

Suggestions

Here are some suggestions which will enable you to control your time while attending a little more to your own needs and the requirements of current objectives.

1. Make sure your energy is channelled in well-thought-out directions:

- Think about Covey's suggestion that time management is not as effective as life leadership. It is important to have a clear life purpose (mission) with prioritized roles and goals.

2. Enlist others to help with the detail work.

- Always ask, "Who else could get this project done instead of me?" If there is any way to hand off, partner, or delegate the task, do so. After all, accomplishing the task is the goal, not who did it.

- If you cannot hire someone else... keep aware of the time required for the detail task.

- Rely on past experiences to anticipate the time needed for new projects.

- Plan far enough ahead, in enough detail, that you can put the project or task on the shelf, at the ready for roll out. Then forget about it and concentrate your energies upon the next priority of the day or week.

- Try to keep notes as you work. These details will help you plan the time needed for future projects. This will be a challenge, as you probably don't enjoy keeping track of such details.

3. Maintain a sense of control by being organized.

- Take the FranklinCovey class and buy a planner.

- Use a daytimer to block out time for all major assignments; then that time is sacrosanct.

- When you delegate important tasks to others, make sure your goals are specific. (This is something you may not be able to do by yourself; you may need a partner of a different type who is able to help you identify specific goals and steps needed to achieve them).

4. Try to maintain balance in your life:

- Take time off for yourself, even though your natural preference is to get work done before play.

- Try hard to live in the present some of the time. Take a few minutes to smell the roses before you're old.

- Try not to beat yourself up if you miss a deadline, but do let others involved know in advance when you need more time and negotiate it into the agreement.

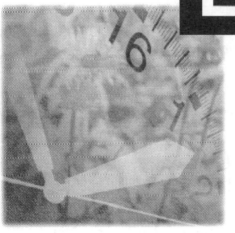

Chapter | 4

ENTP

An Introduction to ENTP

ENTP

If you are an ENTP, are likely to be versatile, full of ideas, and enthusiastic about things which interest you. You are strong in initiative and creative impulse, but not strong in completing projects. You operate by impulsive energy rather than concentrated will power. You can become obsessed or totally absorbed with what interests you, but have difficulty getting things done if they do not interest you.

One of your greatest problems in time management may be in overextending yourself and others. Although you are good at focusing on the big picture and future happenings, you can get so involved in conceptual models that you forget about current realities, and you may not be realistic with regard to how long it can take to put ideas into practice. Your own enthusiasm and tendency to total involvement in a project you like can hamper your sense of timing. Furthermore, you may take on too many projects and too many deadlines, some of which may eventually suffer.

With your visionary enthusiasm for most of life and your relentless drive, you have the potential to break through new frontiers in many areas. But unless you can learn to follow through on your exciting ideas, truly manage concrete details, and overcome your tendency to be distracted by new project directions, you may actually have little to show for all your work.

Here are how six ENTPs are trying to cope with time management issues. These ENTPs are not necessarily typical of their types, but their stories can provide helpful insights and ideas for you and others. Several identify how they make the most of the strengths which result from their type preferences, and several tell how they compensate for their natural weaknesses. Some tell of difficulties yet unsolved. Together they provide some unique ideas and useful suggestions for ENTPs.

Stories, Ideas, & Suggestions

Hal

Q. Tell me about an occasion when you felt really successful in managing your time.

I'm great at managing my time when I have a big, team-oriented, intellectual project I can really sink my teeth into. I can play off the solitary work and the discussions with others. I love to see the streams come together. I see myself as a leader by influence rather than by fiat. I go all out to have my parts done well and to see that all the parts fit well together. I find this role extremely motivating. It's exactly what I want to do, so of course I have no trouble managing my time. I'm able to map out general plans, e.g. a monthly timeline, and get the buy-in of others.

I feel most successful when the projects are large ones and last for weeks or months. Then the day to day ups and downs have less effect, e.g. chairing a one-day conference for engineers, planned for months, organized and run by volunteers; leading the team starting a web site; systems analysis and project management; writing books and manuals; taking academic courses.

Q. Tell me about some of your difficulties in time management.

My difficulties? If I have a lot of little things to do I often feel out of control. I have to write down the simplest things for fear I will forget them. I don't connect things, e.g. I go to the store to get something then later realize I needed something else; I remember I have a meeting next week but am unclear on the day until I suddenly realize I have a conflict. I don't have a good sense of timing on some things, e.g. how long to wait before calling back someone who should have returned my call.

I have difficulty estimating the time it will take to accomplish something. This is probably due to the fact I don't see all the steps clearly. It also has to do with motivation: if I want to do it, the time doesn't matter; if not, all the time in the world wouldn't be enough.

Q. What advice can you offer to others of your type regarding time management?

I'd say to ENTPs: be careful what you sign up for. It's probably going to take you longer than you think. And you may lose interest before you're through. And if you do it well, your 'reward' may be that you get to do it again and again, which you may not want.

Q. What help would you like to get regarding time management from others of your type?

From other ENTPs? Probably I need the help from other types! The ENTPs would just encourage my time-wasting ways -- interesting but irrelevant conversations, speculations, humour, competition, moodiness. But they might affirm the value of my weirdness when my confidence flags, and could at least go forward...

Kartik

Q. Tell me about an occasion when you felt really successful in managing your time.

I feel most successful at managing my time when I 'create time' -- that is, I think of something clever that solves a problem in a much shorter period of time than I thought, which frees up time that I can use to do other things (or maybe nothing at all). I also feel pretty successful at managing my time when my multitasking effectiveness (not necessarily raw efficiency) is high. That's when I'm in the 'zone,' making progress in a wide variety of areas, but it's all getting done effortlessly and, in fact, giving me energy.

Q. Tell me about some of your difficulties in time management.

I'd rather not expound on my difficulties. Suffice it to say, they're just like the ENTP type description points them out to be...

Q. What advice can you offer to others of your type regarding time management?

I've learned a lot about time management by reframing the problem into one of 'life leadership.' Stephen Covey's books like *'First Things First'* have been very insightful in my developing a better understanding of the underlying principles. I don't do a lot of the detail work that he recommends -- I don't use a daytimer, I don't periodically revise a written mission statement.

Instead, I use what I'm most comfortable with, extroverted intuition and introverted thinking. I keep a 'big picture' outlook of what my ultimate goals are in my mind, and connect them dynamically to actions that I'm taking on a day-to-day, even instant-by-instant basis. I look for opportunistic moments in conversations with others (and mailing lists like these) to periodically externalize my tacit thinking into explicit statements.

Some 'tips' that may be helpful to others of the ENTP mindset:

1. Use your dominant time-handling strengths when working with others. Look for opportunities to under-specify time. For example, when asked by someone about setting up a time to talk, first find out whether they're willing to accept 'any time next week' (assuming that you're mostly free next week of course). If so, then you've successfully saved yourself the energy that would otherwise go into making sure that you're in a certain place at a certain time. This works because you can context-switch pretty easily.

2. Develop good working relationships with those who have better logistical skills. Find ways to help them in areas of your strength -- they will then be more likely to value your strengths, and can help you out with detail work. This is a win-win type of situation.

Q. What help would you like to get regarding time management from others of your type?

I'm be curious to hear about other people's philosophy on time management, as well as tips from experience.

Teresa

Successes and difficulties at managing time:

I don't know if I am a typical ENTP, but time management is not one of my strongest suits.

The only time I have felt really successful in time management is when I had so little to do that I was bored. Then I had time to write in my Franklin Planner and set goals, etc. But being bored drives me crazy, I'd rather be so busy that I don't have much extra time. Usually I write what I have scheduled on the month at a glance page of my planner and it rarely makes it to my daily pages. Only when something HAS to get done do I write it on my daily page to do list. And then I don't remember to mark it completed.

Funny, I have had some really detailed oriented jobs. I keep most of my plans in my head and also keep track of details that way. I am very bad at writing things down. I solve these problems by hiring strong SJ types as my assistant. They keep me in line and keep my desk and other paperwork organized. Plus they follow through for me, my least favourite part.

I am successful as I am, although sometimes others worry about my time management abilities when they watch me work. Once I they have seen the quality of the services I provide, then they no longer are concerned. I push that working up to the deadline as far as I can get.

My best advice...

Choose your assistants well, make sure they complement your strengths.

Help from others...

I'd love to hear what else you learn.

Steve

Some of the difficulties that I have in managing time, are mostly
concerned with how relative time is to me. When I am interested in
something, time has no meaning for me. I often become lost in new and
exciting things that I find. The internet is a large waster of time for me.
I go online looking for one thing, and then minutes into being online, I am
looking at something else. I also love to gab, and if I am having an
interesting conversation I usually think nothing of putting off whatever
I have planned next to continue that conversation. It often becomes a
problem when people are expecting me at a certain time, or when my boss
is irritated cause I am late often. The harsh part is, that I don't think
people that are late are rude. I can't classify it that way, because I have
no problem making myself late. I usually tell myself that if someone else is
going to be mad, then they'll be mad. Oh well. I am never really successful
in managing my time. Only after I read Stephen Covey's habits of highly
effective people did I start to use a planner. I have found it really good
when I plan events far off into the future. Like I am returning to college
after a seven year absence, and I have been planning that for about a year.
Everything that I have planned has been done without a hitch. So I guess
I am good, looking into the future and planning but if I plan a day, it never
goes the way I planned because I get so easily sidetracked and the
individual minutes mean nothing to me.

Advice to other ENTPs:

The only advice I could offer is to make sure that an ENTP plans for the
future. Otherwise nothing will get done.

Mary

Q. *Tell me about an occasion when you felt really successful in managing your time.*

I used to feel most successful managing my time when I was living and working a 'J' life. I was employed full-time, taught two nights each week, and completed a masters degree in a year and a half. That felt like success.

Q. *Tell me about some of your difficulties in time management.*

The difficulties I have experienced are directly related to the emergence of my 'P' preference. I find it stressful when, having been so successful at time management in the past, I now let things slide, or forget them, or don't care enough to follow through on them. I haven't had a significant emotional experience where my (new) easy-going approach has created an extreme difficulty in my life; however, there are times when I feel more stress and that nagging feeling that I have forgotten something. When I embrace what I believe is my natural preference for 'P' (I believe my previous job situation truly drove my 'J' preference), I do find that it has impacted my ability to do a thousand things at once successfully!

Advice to other ENTPs:

Don't be too relaxed in your approach to getting things done. Entertain your 'J' preference to the degree you need to ensure you don't worry--your 'T' preference generates that worry so be kind to yourself as well. Spend time alone each day to plan what you will accomplish, then go out and interact with everyone to get things done. Delegate what you can as soon as you know it needs to be done (hopefully to an ISTJ who does a great job of accomplishing those types of things that we could care less about!). Remember that the big picture only shows you where you're going, but you need to use your logic and analysis to identify the steps needed to get there! Realize that you are not above tasks that need to be done and just DO It!

Diane

Q. *Tell me about an occasion when you felt really successful in managing your time.*

I don't have one specific occasion in mind. But in general, it is when I get a lot done, and done well, with efficient use of time. It usually means working at a fast pace, feeling productive and competent.

Q. *Tell me about some of your difficulties in time management.*

Things often take longer than I think they will so I get frustrated when there is less time left after the task is completed than I expected or when I don't accomplish what I set out to at the beginning of the day. I also get distracted sometimes and may do several other things that caught my attention before getting back to complete the first thing I started. Another difficulty is that I don't always prioritize what is really more important to get done at a certain time so may spend time on what I felt like doing more than what really should have been done sooner.

Q. *What advice can you offer to others of your type regarding time management?*

If you do that task that you like least or tend to procrastinate - it will actually help you get things done quicker, more positively and save energy in the long run.

It helps to prioritize what is more important and start there. Always allow for things to take longer than you think they will. This goes double when other people are involved.

Q. *What help would you like to get regarding time management from others of your type?*

Other hints that people have found helpful.

Discussion

As might be expected, the ENTP responses were remarkable for their wit, originality, and cleverness. At first, some of their suggestions didn't actually make sense to me (an INFP), but when I sent back their responses to each other for feedback, I found out that the very suggestions which seemed most confusing to me, were most applauded by them!

Although some of the contributors were able to tell at least one time management success story, almost all seemed prone to a common difficulty: getting distracted or diverted and not completing what they start.

This was not surprising. According to type theory, the force that animates ENTPs is an intuitive vision of possibilities. ENTPs are irresistibly drawn to questions and ideas, and find themselves continually plunging into new options. Life is a game, with one exciting challenge after another.

Since the challenge and excitement of a never-ending array of new ideas and possibilities is what gives meaning to their lives, it would be heartless for any time management consultant to advise ENTPs to improve their time management by asking them to ignore the new possibilities which continually come to mind. This would be like asking them to avoid life!

The contributors to this study seemed to understand this. When asked to provide suggestions for others like themselves, they offered only ideas which would enable ENTPs to appreciate work and life in their own way, while coping with the demands of the world around them.

Since they know the distractions are not going to go away (thank goodness, since new options, questions, and possibilities are the driving force of their lives!), the best thing to do is to work around them:

"Be careful what you sign up for. It's probably going to take you longer than you think. And you may lose interest before you're through. And if you do it well, your 'reward' may be that you get to do it again and again, which you may not want."

Since new possibilities and options are always around, you simply have to keep on track in spite of them. "It helps to prioritize what is more important and start there, and always allow for things to take longer than you think they will. That goes double when other people are involved."

ENTPs want life and work to be intellectually stimulating and they want recognition for their clever ideas. Unfortunately, if they lose interest in a project as soon as the tedious details have to be completed, and move on to more exciting new options, no one will ever see the results of their efforts. The ENTP contributors were aware of this problem, so they suggested: "Develop good relationships with those who have better skill in doing the detail work." "Choose your assistants well; find ones who complement your strengths." "Delegate what you can as soon as you know it needs to be done (hopefully to an ISTJ who does a great job of accomplishing those types of things that we could care less about!)." For those ENTPs who are not yet in a position where they can off-load some of their undesired tasks to others, there was some rather forceful advice: "Accept the fact that you have to do some things you don't like to do in order to move on to things you do want to do." "Don't be too relaxed in your approach to getting things done." "Realize that you are not above tasks that need to be done and just DO it!" (Though one ENTP later said that this sounded hopelessly dreary.)

The ENTP contributors did not offer many ideas for detailed planning, because sticking to a schedule does not accommodate the surge of creativity and total immersion that their own work style can offer. You will recall Kartik's statement: "When I am in the 'zone'... it's getting done effortlessly and, in fact, giving me energy."

There were, however, a few practical suggestions to help ENTPs avoid getting into a bind, as these people know their own vulnerabilities! "Try to develop a stronger internal connection between current tasks and your 'big picture' vision." "Remember that the big picture only shows you where you're going, but you need to use your logic and analysis to identify the steps needed to get there!"

As mentioned earlier, type should not be an excuse for behaviour. Rather, an understanding of a person's natural preferences can be helpful in the development of an effective style which embraces whatever provides the driving force and gives life its joy and meaning. The contributors, by recognizing what gives zest to their own lives, were able to offer some useful suggestions to help ENTPs to be more effective time managers while still being themselves. And if all else fails, they said: "Actively seek out positions where your talents are appreciated and you don't have to spend a lot of energy on the tedious details you don't enjoy."

Helping ENTPs Find their Own Way

Characteristics and behaviours which could be expected of an ENTP

- versatile

- full of ideas

- enthusiastic about things which interest you

- strong in initiative

- creative

- not strong in completing projects

- can become obsessed or totally absorbed in something of interest

- have difficulty getting things done if they are not interesting

- may overextend yourself and others

- good at focusing on the big picture and future happenings

- may forget about current realities

- may not be realistic in estimating time required

- may take on too many projects

Driving forces
Irresistibly drawn to developing, improvising and adapting new ideas and possibilities.

Problems *most* likely to occur
Getting distracted or diverted and not completing things.

Solutions *least* likely to be followed
Ignore the new possibilities that come to mind.

Suggestions

Here are some suggestions to help you do things in your own way while coping with the demands of the world around you.

1. Choose your projects carefully.

- Be careful what you sign up for, it's probably going to take you longer than you think. And you may lose interest before you're through.

2. Get help if you can.

- Develop good relationships with those who have better skill in doing the detail work.

- Choose your assistants well; find ones who complement your strengths.

- Delegate what you can as soon as you know it needs to be done (Hopefully to an ISTJ who does a great job of accomplishing those types of things that we could care less about!).

3. Know that there are going to be distractions.

- It helps to prioritize what is more important and start there, and always allow for things to take longer than you think they will. That goes double when other people are involved.

4. Do a little more planning.

- Spend time alone each day to plan what you will accomplish, then go out and interact with everyone to get things done.

- Try to develop a stronger internal connection between current tasks and your 'big picture' vision.

- Remember that the big picture only shows you where you're going, but you need to use your logic and analysis to identify the steps needed to get there!

5. Sometimes self-discipline is necessary.

- If you do that task that you like least (or tend to procrastinate), it will actually help you get things done quicker, more positively and save energy in the long run.

- Accept the fact that you have to do some things you don't like to do in order to move on to things you do want to do.

- Don't be too relaxed in your approach to getting things done.

6. If necessary, consider alternatives.

- Actively seek out positions where your talents are appreciated and you don't have to spend a lot of energy on the tedious details you don't enjoy.

Chapter | 5

ESFJ

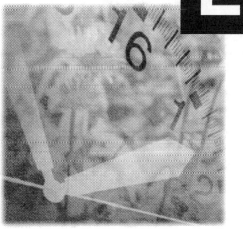

An Introduction to ESFJ

If you are an ESFJ, you are likely to be persevering and conscientious. You are probably orderly even in small matters and expect others to be orderly also. You are matter-of-fact and practical, and usually like things to be settled in the conventional way. You have a clear sense of right and wrong.

You probably prefer a work environment which is stable and orderly, where tasks are defined and everyone knows what is to be done, by who, and by what date. You have a strong sense of responsibility.

Generally, you respect rules and authority and handle daily operations efficiently, promptly and courteously. You are well organized, and usually have a place for everything and everything in its place.

You like to be seen as thorough, reliable, and responsive. You can work well with other people. However, if expectations or priorities are not made clear, you may feel uncomfortable. Sometimes your sense of responsibility can cause you to get overloaded with work. Your commitment and loyalty to people or organizations may cause you to forget about your own needs. Lack of cooperation from co-workers can be extremely upsetting.

Time management is probably not a great problem for you, but even ESFJs can have difficulties in certain circumstances. I asked five ESFJs how they try to cope with time management. These ESFJs are not necessarily typical of their types, but their stories can provide helpful insights and ideas for you and others. Several identify how they make the most of the strengths which result from their type preferences, and several tell how they compensate for their natural weaknesses. Some tell of difficulties yet unsolved. Together they provide some unique ideas and useful suggestions for ESFJs.

Stories, Ideas, & Suggestions

Janet

Q. Tell me about an occasion when you felt really successful in managing your time.

I can't think of any one situation (in which I have been successful in time management) since everything I do relates to deadlines - but one time when I feel successful is Sunday evenings when I have successfully planned my work projects and prioritized, kids' activities are taken care of, etc... I know my week will go smoothly.

Q. Tell me about some of your difficulties in time management.

Main difficulty is that I take on too much. I tend to believe that I can do anything and because I enjoy helping others I will agree to give them my time to finish their projects. Also, I have difficulties delegating work. I'm not 100% sure as to why, either because I think I can do the best job or I think I can handle the time constraints. I do not like missing deadlines and I will work all hours of the night to meet a deadline - and due to the nature of my work, deadlines are a constant happening.

Difficulties also arise between my family life and my work life. I have four children (ages three to eleven) and a partnership. I am extremely dedicated to both and have difficulties cutting work short when I need to go home, likewise getting extra work done in the evening once I am home with the children. I suppose I would say that my greatest difficulty in time management is there aren't enough hours in the day and I wish sometimes I didn't have to sleep.

Q. What advice can you offer to others of your type regarding time management?

The best advise I would give to other ESFJs - you can not do everything. Think about yourself first and remember to only take on what you honestly have time for. i.e. Prioritize your time, your projects, and your life. Remember not to be concerned only about letting other people down but letting yourself down too.

Q. *What help would you like to get regarding time management from others of your type?*

I'd like to get some practical advice on how to relax! I have so much going on in my life, I am always thinking of what I have to do, what I need to finish, where I need to go, what I need to organize, etc. I have real difficulties putting everything down and watching a movie. i.e. I'll iron while I watch TV so I'm not wasting my time. I'll clean the kitchen when I'm talking on the phone, clean the bathroom when the kids are in the tub, etc... I can only relax when I'm on a vacation, away from the house and away from the office.

John

Q. *Tell me about an occasion when you felt really successful in managing your time.*

I feel successful whenever I'm real busy and manage to get everything done on time. Most recent specific and significant example might be my hosting of my daughter's wedding last fall. Daughter did most of the work, but I managed a lot of the scheduling, running around, and budgeting myself.

Q. *Tell me about some of your difficulties in time management.*

My difficulties include frittering time away on low priority activities such as reading junk mail.

Advice to other ESFJs:

Making a list helps. I tend to avoid this whenever possible. But the act of writing down a number of activities in a list insures that I make best use of my time and travels. Helps me to see relative priorities, too.

Valerie

Successes and difficulties at managing time:

I think I qualify as having a 'J' mouth and 'P' behaviour! Certainly that would explain some of my delay in replying to your request. I have excellent intentions, and I would like to help you out, but my time management is severely deficient these days. Then, I reason, perhaps it is just type development (I am 47)... exercising those skills of flexibility, open options... or maybe its just wanting to do too much, which my type is prone to do in the service of others. But I have not felt successful in time management on any occasion recent enough to remember in any detail at all. Perhaps this Christmas I will get all the gifts wrapped before Christmas Eve - I managed last year, but using the very last minute (not stereotypically 'J'? huh?!)

My day planner is effective in keeping track of the things I want or need to do until I cross them off because they no longer need to be done, or because they WERE done - probably because they HAD to be done.

Advice to other ESFJs:

Continually prioritize, to keep from skipping what you feel is important.

Help from other ESFJs:

This could come by way of NOT asking me if I could do anything... I know I can say NO but then how is cooperation attained, and how can I expect others to do MY bidding?! No, pressure is all me... and now I have to write a newsletter article that I really don't feel I am qualified to write, but everyone else is so busy, and no one wants to write it, and... why am I on this committee if I don't want to do stuff... END OF BRAIN DUMP. Sharon, good luck with your project. There are so many other issues involved in behaviour, type is sometimes hard to sort out... I do know that ESFJ IS my type. Ticking off accomplishments is important to me, but so is that LAST MINUTE and beyond! I am, like other successful individuals, excellent at getting to work and appointments on time (I'm a marriage and family therapist) - but I know how to drive fast! Be well.

Ann

Q. Tell me about an occasion when you felt really successful in managing your time.

I became a director for one division of an organization a few months ago. My predecessor was with this organization for nine years and carried much of the knowledge and structure of the position in her head. The nature of this position is very deadline oriented. I found the best way to focus my energies was to develop a check list of every task, some very basic, that needed to be completed and the date by which it needed to be completed. This helped me to stay focused on priorities and ensure that nothing was overlooked. This system allowed me to have a better picture of the overall process and I discovered many steps along the way that could be combined, deleted or delegated. This has allowed me to take on several projects that in the past were not the responsibility of this particular position.

Q. Tell me about some of your difficulties in time management.

My difficulties arise sometimes when I do not check my lists often enough. As I have gained experience in this position I have grown more confident and often rely on my memory rather than the check list or notes. I find that gets me into trouble because I may do something twice or do something that does not need to be done, or I may lose sight of priorities.

Q. What advice can you offer to others of your type regarding time management?

My advice to others would be to set your priorities for the day, week and/or month and stay focused on them. Don't allow 'the squeaky wheel to always get the grease.'

Martha

Hi!

Best wishes with your research! I'm happy to participate. I'm just writing this on the spot without thinking before responding so I may write now and then write more later. I like to respond right away to requests like yours on e-mail to assure you that I received it and am interested. Is this an ESFJ approach or what!

I find myself always wanting to do little detail jobs first while I ponder about the bigger projects as I am doing the little pieces. I find I need to work on those little pieces to eventually come to the big project with enough concrete pieces to see a big pattern and picture.

Sometimes I am struck by a strange phenomenon of wanting to work on something that is due - a presentation or paper or project - in the far distant future and not work on the immediate project needs. It is an interesting phenomenon to me as I do care a lot about having things organized ahead of time, but I find at this point in my career and life, that I am just getting things done at the last minute. I ponder on ideas for a long time as I am working on other things, and then it all comes together at the end. Somehow! Usually very late at night.

I guess I find myself collecting and collecting (ideas and materials) as I prepare for a presentation or writing and then I pull it all together at the very end. I am finding enjoyment and difficulty in working with others on projects. The good thing is that I am forced to work ahead and step by step on projects when I am working with someone else. The bad thing is that I find myself putting the finishing touches on the projects in my own way at the very end. Again late at night. I do think it is a function of having a lot on my plate right now.

Hope this helps. Glad to have it shared and to receive information from others on tips and strategies.

Discussion

As might be expected, the ESFJ contributors all seemed warm, friendly and willing to help others by participating in this project. In their stories, many mentioned the need to care for others as part of their workload.

Almost all of them were able to tell at least one successful time management story. But they seemed prone to a common difficulty: saying 'no' to requests for help. Many seemed to feel that there were not enough hours in the day.

This was not surprising. According to type theory, the force that animates ESFJs is the need to respond to others and have things settled. ESFJs are irresistibly drawn to meeting others' needs.

Since responding to the needs of others is such a driving force for their lives, it would not make sense to advise ESFJs to shut themselves away where they can get their work done, because other people are such an intrinsic part of their work and lives. Nor would it make too much sense to ask them to off-load work to others. This does not come naturally for them, and would usually make them feel uncomfortable.

The contributors to this study seemed to understand this. When asked to provide suggestions for others like themselves, they offered only ideas which would enable ESFJs to respond to the needs of others, while attending a little more to their own needs as well. They suggested: "Don't be just concerned about letting other people down; be concerned about letting yourself down too." "Remember that sometimes you really do have to say 'no'. And others may have to say 'no' to you too!" "Don't get overloaded." "Set your priorities for the day, week, and month and stay focused on them. Don't allow the 'squeaky wheel to always get the grease."

ESFJs know, deep in their hearts, that they are going to keep responding to the needs of others and that there will always be people needing help from them. This is, after all, what life is all about. Since ESFJs are driven to respond to the needs of others and that requires time (you can't rock a baby fast!), they have to be well organized. This is why some of the suggestions included: "Prioritize your time, your projects and your life." "Make lists or write down activities that need to be done." "Check your lists frequently..." One contributor said she was interested in learning more specific tips and strategies. Probably other ESFJs would also appreciate more detailed, tried-and-true tips for more efficient practices specific to the needs of their workplace or home.

As mentioned earlier, type should not be an excuse for behaviour. Rather, an understanding of a person's natural preferences can be helpful in the development of an effective style which embraces whatever provides the driving force and gives life its meaning. The contributors offered some useful suggestions to help ESFJs to continue to serve well while not getting overworked.

Helping ESFJs Find their Own Way

Characteristics and behaviours which could be expected of an ESFJ:

- persevering
- conscientious
- orderly even in small matters
- matter-of-fact
- practical
- usually like things to be settled in the conventional way
- clear sense of right and wrong
- prefer a work environment which is stable and orderly
- want tasks to be clearly defined
- have a strong sense of responsibility
- respect rules and authority
- handle daily operations efficiently, promptly and courteously

- well organized
- usually have a place for everything and everything in its place
- like to be seen as thorough, reliable, and responsive
- can work well with other people
- may feel uncomfortable if expectations or priorities are not made clear
- may get overloaded with work
- loyal to people or organization
- may forget about own needs
- find lack of cooperation from co-workers upsetting

Driving forces
To serve well.

Problems *most* likely to occur
Getting overloaded with work.

Solutions *least* likely to be followed
Shut yourself away from people so you can get your work done.

Suggestions

Here are some suggestions that may help you do your work and still help others when necessary, while attending a little more to your own needs as well.

1. Prioritize.

- Make lists or write down activities that need to be done. This will insure that you are making the best use of your time, and help you to see relative priorities.
- Prioritize your work projects and your home life.
- When you set your priorities for the day, week and month, stay focused on them. Don't allow the 'squeaky wheel to always get the grease.'
- Check your lists frequently, even when you think you have everything in your memory, so that you don't skip anything that you feel is really important.

2. Be aware of your own time limitations.

- Take on only as much as you honestly have time for.
- Don't just be concerned about letting other people down; be concerned about letting yourself down too.
- Remember that sometimes you really do have to say 'no.' And others may have to say 'no' to you too!

3. Find out specific tips and strategies from others who have experience in your job.

Chapter | 6

ESFP

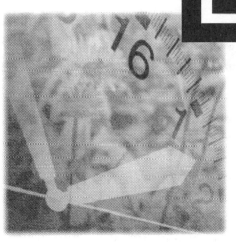

An Introduction to ESFP

If you are an ESFP, you are likely to be good at coming up with practical ways of doing things. You learn from experience and on the job. You are friendly and tolerant of others, and can easily adapt to changing situations to make things run smoothly. You prefer to work without an exact plan, 'winging it' and dealing with situations as they arise.

You are generally light-hearted, lively and enthusiastic, and enjoy working with other people, preferably in a workspace which is comfortable and attractive. You appreciate having a variety of creative things to do and enjoy seeing immediate results of your efforts. You want work to be fun and ever-changing.

You believe people are important and tend to organize around people's needs. As a result, there may be delays or distractions and you may find yourself running late and needing to apologise. Others may think you are disorganized.

I asked five ESFPs how they try to cope with time management. These ESFPs are not necessarily typical of their types, but their stories can provide helpful information for you and others. Several identify how they make the most of the strengths which result from their type preferences, and several tell how they compensate for their natural weaknesses. Some tell of difficulties yet unsolved. Together they provide some unique ideas and useful suggestions for ESFPs.

Stories, Ideas, & Suggestions

Nancy

Q. Tell me about an occasion when you felt really successful in managing your time.

My five-year-old grandchild visited me for one week, we ate, slept, and did everything together. I had to co-ordinate her time for fun stuff, while I was at work. A five year old needs full time supervision. It all worked out beautifully and I wasn't late for work once!

Q. Tell me about some of your difficulties in time management.

Because I enjoy a diversified job and lifestyle, I have a hard time meeting paper-like deadlines. For example, my bills are paid one day late, friends get birthday cards one day late, if I sign up for a class or event, I'm usually last minute. I don't know how to end a phone conversation with a friend who wants to keep on talking, without hurting her feelings.

Q. What advice can you offer to others of your type regarding time management?

Try to follow set patterns and guidelines on projects, no matter if you enjoy the project or not.

Bruce

Q. Tell me about an occasion when you felt really successful in managing your time.

I am pretty good at time management when I have committed to a deadline. I find a way to accomplish what I need to in a specified period of time. I am working on a large project right now which must be finished in six months and I feel I have it under control.

Q. Tell me about some of your difficulties in time management.

Of course one of the difficulties is procrastination. Even though I feel comfortable in this project I am checking e-mail, responding to you, etc. I am good at being distracted because I have so many things I like to do.

Q. What advice can you offer to others of your type regarding time management?

I often will create a deadline to get myself motivated. I don't like to fall short of a commitment or let people down so I'll use this to help myself perform better.

Q. What help would you like to get regarding time management from others of your type?

I am curious of the problems others encounter and the ideas they have to help themselves - particularly ESFPs. Good luck.

John

Successes and difficulties at managing time:

First of all, I really fit the typical ESFP profile and have the strengths and weaknesses of that style. My difficulties are primarily due to scheduling too many activities and have difficulty saying NO. Scheduling 'too much' causes me to overload and push hard to get everything completed.
I typically like to work on short term projects and don't do well with long range planning. I tend to put things off and do them closer to their due date. Next year is another millennium for me and I will worry about those items later. This creates some stress in those that like to see work completed on a programmed schedule. I am, however, very flexible and adaptable. I am good at handling multiple projects... as long as they are short term. I can do the long range projects but they are not my first choice. I do well with 'attention to detail' activities and even large projects of a logistics type. (I spent 21 years in the Air Force as a Pilot so that might shed some light on my information).

Suggestions for other ESFPs:

As far as advice I would only say to work on the things I have mentioned earlier.

Help needed:

I work as an organizational development consultant and do a lot of training and development work also. I am certified in Covey, DDI, Learning International and many others. I also teach time management... I just need to practice what I preach.

I hope this is enough information. If you would like more just let me know. Chow.

Jackie

Hi Sharon, I am actually home for a day or two before I am off travelling again. In answer to your questions:

Q. *Tell me about an occasion when you felt really successful in managing your time.*

One of my best time management situations was a workshop I was doing for our INTJ salesman. He had arranged for me to run a sales training workshop for 30 sales people that worked for six different companies that compete against each other. Because I knew Frank (our Salesman) was an INTJ I knew he had to have things organized and done early. I actually had all the MBTI results scored, the itinerary planned and typed and all the handouts prepared a month in advance and everything sent to Frank by courier so he had it in his truck ready to take to the workshop. This was a major feat for me to have everything done this early. The real reason I did it was because of my feeling preference wanting to make sure our INTJ salesman was comfortable and happy. What I didn't tell Frank, was that I had no idea which games I was going to play at the workshop. I took a variety of games with me and just flew by the seat of my pants and played whichever ones felt good at the time.

Q. Tell me about some of your difficulties in time management.

My three greatest challenges are:

1) not being able to say 'no' to people so I am always offering to do things for people that I really don't have time to do.

2) I am notorious for filling my plate way too full, because I try to do everything and I always plan way more than can possibly fit in a day. For this reason I am almost always 10-15 minutes late. To get around this I never tell someone an exact time I will be there. I always give myself a half hour leeway. i.e. I tell people I will be there between 8:00 and 8:30. That way I don't put the extra stress on myself to meet a time commitment I know I can't.

3) I find it very hard to stay focused on one task. If I am in the middle of something at work, and someone comes in and asks me for something, I will drop everything to do that thing. The next thing I know I have ten things on the go and they are all in various stages of completion. I get bored with projects very easily and I really have to force myself to finish them. I come up with great ideas, start them and then get bored. I have three sweaters sitting in a basket in my living room in various stages of completion. One of them has been there for about three years.

Q. What advice can you offer to others of your type regarding time management?

Make yourself finish things, it actually feels good to complete something.

When you decide to do something, just go do it, and don't second guess yourself, because if you keep thinking about something, you will always come up with a better plan and the thing never gets done.

My next advice is learn how to say 'no' and not feel guilty about it.

Thirdly, use a 'to do list' of some description. It doesn't have to be an elaborate time management system. Just a piece of paper that you can write things down on and prioritize them to get them done. Also learn to tell people you can't do it right know, and then make a note of it and actually finish what you are doing first. That one is almost impossible for me because of my feeling preference always wanting to make everyone else happy.

Sharon, I hope this is helpful! If you need anything else, just e-mail me.

David

Successes and difficulties at managing time:

During tax season there are many issues that can remain outstanding while clients look for information. Having a steady flow, to the work process while arranging enough time to follow up with 'open' files and still complete the task by the April 30th deadline is a real 'rush'. When I feel most successful is when I establish a time line for completion of a task, and then I beat the estimated time. It is like a competition to see if I can do better than I think I can.

I am easily sidetracked, and find myself working on several tasks at one time. This causes frustration when tasks are not completed according to my estimated time.

My time is controlled by others who are unstructured. I don't know how I can help others be respectful of time management.

Advice for others: Use the three pile method.

Pile 1: Not interesting, very urgent projects

Pile 2: Very interesting, not urgent projects

Pile 3: Not interesting, not urgent project.

For every two out of pile #1, reward yourself by doing one out of pile #2. Ignore pile #3 until they fall into one of the other two categories.

Thank you for the opportunity to help.

Discussion

As might be expected, the ESFPs provided friendly, matter-of-fact replies.

Almost all of the ESFPs were able to tell at least one successful time management story. But they seemed prone to a common difficulty: getting distracted.

This was not surprising. According to type theory, the force that animates ESFPs is the need to respond to current situations. ESFPs are drawn to attending to human and situational needs, often in a fun and lively way.

Since responding to the needs of the moment is such a driving force for their lives, it would be useless for anyone to advise ESFPs to plan carefully and stick with the plan, ignoring everything else. This would be like asking them to ignore life!

The contributors to this study seemed to understand this. When asked to provide suggestions for others like themselves, they offered only suggestions which would enable ESFPs to respond to the demands of the moment, while still meeting required deadlines. They suggested: "Avoid being late by not telling people the exact time you will be there." "Give yourself a half-hour leeway for appointments."

The ESFPs feel they should meet deadlines and finish things, especially if others are involved because they don't want to let other people down. So they suggest: "Create a deadline to get yourself motivated. If you have a commitment to people you won't want to let them down, and you can use this to help yourself perform better."

Since ESFPs so much like to enjoy life in the here-and-now, it's hard to get down to doing something less interesting. Sometimes, they realize, it's just a little more self-discipline that's needed: "Try to follow set patterns and guidelines on projects, no matter if you enjoy the project or not." "Make yourself finish things; it actually feels good to complete something."

To deal with distractions, they said: "Learn to not feel guilty about saying 'no' to tasks which are going to overload you." "Learn to tell people you can't do it right now, then make a note of it and actually finish what you are doing first. (Try it, although this will be hard, because of your preference to make other people happy.)"

The ESFPs recognized that sometimes tools are needed to keep on track, but they do not like planning; they prefer "winging it." So even the suggestion of a 'to do list' was made with some qualification to make it more palatable for this type. "Use a 'to do list' of some description. It doesn't have to be an elaborate time management system, just a piece of paper that you can write things down on and prioritize them to get them done." One contributor offered a three-pile system, based on prioritizing very urgent (but uninteresting) projects over not urgent (but interesting) projects, using the second pile as a reward for doing the first pile. A third pile contained uninteresting, not urgent things. He encouraged ESFP types to just ignore this pile until it fell into one of the other two categories. This system might fit comfortably into the ESFP's preferred lifestyle.

As mentioned earlier, type should not be an excuse for behaviour. Rather, an understanding of a person's natural preferences can be helpful in the development of an effective style which embraces whatever provides the driving force and gives life its meaning. The contributors offered some useful suggestions to help ESFPs to be more effective time managers while still being themselves.

Helping ESFPs Find their Own Way

Characteristics and behaviours which could be expected of an ESFP

- practical
- learn from experience
- friendly
- tolerant of others
- adaptable
- prefer to work without an exact plan
- like to deal with situations as they arise
- light-hearted

- lively
- enjoy working with people
- like to have a variety of creative things to do
- like to see immediate results
- want work to be fun
- enjoy change
- tend to organize around people's needs

Driving forces
The desire to live in the moment, to meet human and situational needs in a fun and lively way.

Problems *most* likely to occur
Getting distracted.

Solutions *least* likely to be followed
Plan carefully and stick with the plan.

Suggestions

Here are some suggestions which will enable you to respond to new situations which come up and still meet your required deadlines.

1. Find ways to motivate yourself to get a task done.

- Create a deadline. If you have a commitment to people you won't want to let them down, and you can use that to help yourself perform better.
- Make yourself finish things; it actually feels good to complete something.

2. Find systems which work for you.

- Follow set patterns and guidelines, no matter if you enjoy the project or not.
- Try a three pile method for your work.

Pile 1: Not interesting, very urgent projects

Pile 2: Very interesting, not urgent projects

Pile 3: Not interesting, not urgent project.

For every two out of pile #1, reward yourself by doing one out of pile #2. Ignore pile #3 until they fall into one of the other two categories.

- Use a 'to do list' of some description. It doesn't have to be an elaborate time management system, just a piece of paper that you can write things down on and prioritize them to get them done.

3. Reduce distractions

- Learn to not feel guilty about saying 'no' to tasks which are going to overload you.
- Learn to tell people you can't do it right now, then make a note of it and actually finish what you are doing first. (Try it, although this will be hard, because of your preference to make other people happy).

4. Know that no matter how hard you try, there will still be some unexpected needs which come up.

- Avoid being late by not telling people the exact time you will be there.
- Give yourself a half-hour leeway for appointments.

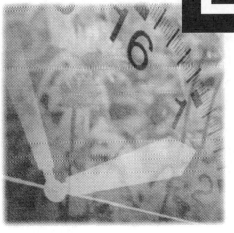

Chapter 7

ESTJ

An Introduction to ESTJ

If you are an ESTJ, you are probably practical and realistic. You like to achieve immediate, tangible and visible results. You enjoy getting things organized and done.

You probably prefer work in an environment which is stable and orderly where everyone expects that goals will be achieved according to plan and on time. You attend to every detail, or give precise instructions to others to do so. You value efficiency; it is important to you that things be done right the first time. You don't like to waste time questioning things which don't matter. The most important thing is getting on with the job.

You expect the organization to support its workers in achieving their tasks; when it fails to do so, when systems malfunction or expectations are ambiguous or unclear, or the process is stalled by others just standing around, you find this extremely disappointing or stressful. You take your work seriously and expect others to do so too. Sometimes your strong sense of responsibility may cause you to end up taking on too much of the burden yourself.

You don't like surprises and changes in plans unless they make sense in the long run. You like to set a goal and make detailed plans around it. In a well structured, smooth-running workplace, you probably have no difficulty completing tasks correctly and on time. But you may run into problems if other people fail to do their part, or if unexpected circumstances arise.

I asked five ESTJs how they try to cope with time management. These ESTJs are not necessarily typical of their types, but their stories can provide helpful information for you and others. Several identify how they make the most of the strengths which result from their type preferences, and several tell how they compensate for their natural weaknesses. Together they provide some unique ideas and useful suggestions for ESTJs.

Stories, Ideas, & Suggestions

Bill

Let me start with a summary of things I do on a daily basis to manage time, what difficulties I have (or better still what 'flips my switch') and some items of advice.

Things I do on a daily basis:

1. Make a list of tasks or things to do for the day...

2. Or when required, when they are due, i.e. a deadline.

3. Prioritize - important things first, not a first-in and first-out approach.

4. Cross-off the list when complete - this makes you feel good.

5. This is done daily, either in the morning or before leaving work at night. It can and is updated during the day as required.

6. If I am doing several projects at the same time, I have different lists of tasks to be accomplished.

7. I integrate the lists to see if I can accomplish several tasks at the same time or setting, i.e. get some synergy.

Difficulties at managing time:

1. When communications break down between task or project team and it causes rework or recycling or reviewing what needs to be done

2. Major changes to previously planned tasks.

3. Lack of support on the front-end of planning or on the follow-on work when it is a serial process.

4. There are probably others, not coming to me at this time.

Advice for ESTJ's:

1. Don't panic!

2. Don't get frustrated, if you do, please recover ASAP.

3. Overextend yourself to communicate, ask for help, or offer help.

4. Look seriously at the changes in or impact to your time, these may be a benefit rather than a reason to panic.

Andre

Q. Tell me about a time when you were successful in time management.

I have been responsible for the delivery of a leadership course for three years. I had to prepare the whole thing way in advance as the participants had to complete two questionnaires prior to the delivery. Also, making sure that all was ready in time for the first day (facilities, course manuals and hand-outs, etc...). Mind you, I had help from an Administrative Assistant who also had other responsibilities... sometimes having to manage his/her time too. I always started with a meeting two months prior the course's first day to distribute the questionnaires and explain what to do. (I had to tell them how to manage it... They were not all ESTJs). The average participation was of 20 people and the course was a five day exercise.

But listen, outside of work, this past Saturday... Before Winter hits us, I had to finish painting part of the house, exterior. I also had to prepare the swimming pool for winter and get rid of a lot of leaves on the front lawn. Started at 9:00 a.m. While the pool was emptying itself slowly, I started painting on one side of the house. Then, I stopped the pool's motor and went on painting the other side of the house. Once this was done, store away the paint and cleaning the paint brushes, I finish my job with the swimming pool, you know... storing the whole kit. Then, I pick up the leaves on the front lawn and a bit in the yard next to the pool. By the time this was all done, it was 2:00 p.m. It was time to stop as it started raining. Believe or not, I also vacuumed the house... and then took a shower. It was then 4:00 p.m. I was very satisfied with my day's work...

Q. Tell me about some difficulties you have had in time management.

I do not have a lot of difficulties in managing my time. I've always planned ahead and most of the time... it works well. When I do things (work or social activities) with procrastinators or people who change their minds too often, I have a problem with managing my time. I will from time to time 'press' others to 'move' a bit faster, but I know others are not all like me. When people take the time to explain as clearly as possible what they want, I can manage my time easily.

Q. What advice can you offer to people of your type?

The best way to manage our time is to be well organized in what we do. Get rid of unnecessary stuff and concentrate on important things. I manage to place/store whatever I'm working with the minute I'm finished using it. This way, should I need to work with it later on, I do not lose time in searching for it. For example, my files are always up to date and stored at the right place. Should I or somebody else need information, I'm ready. Also, once everything is stored away... you find yourself with more time to do other stuff. Should I find myself in a 'very rush' situation, I take a deep breath, look at the situation... and go about it.

Mickey

Q. Tell me about a time when you were successful in time management.

The problem with question #1 is, I hardly ever feel that I have successfully managed my time! Life is a never-ending battle of lists for me. I have a 'things to do' list in every room of my house, it seems. To answer this question honestly, I always feel as though I am battling the clock and therefore, never have felt successful in time management.

Q. Tell me about some difficulties you have had in time management.

Some of the difficulties I have encountered:

- Going into too much detail on some things and neglecting others.

- Not prioritizing my efforts into accomplishing the most important tasks at hand.

- Lack of organization.

Q. What advice can you offer to people of your type?

Focus, Focus, Focus on the task at hand!

Michael

Successes at managing time:

I feel the most successful in time management when I prioritize my family, then the rest of the world. Being an advocate of Covey I try to keep things in 'Quadrant 2'. I don't let the emergencies of others dictate my priorities. So, I feel the most successful when I maximize the time with my family.

Difficulties at managing time:

The difficulties lie in letting others set your priorities. Staying out of 'Quadrant 1' where I am constantly putting out fires. Therefore, I work hard at setting my priorities. The difficulty also lies when I don't take the time to schedule my priorities, instead I prioritize my schedule. This means to constantly play catch up with what my priorities are.

Advice to other ESTJs:

As Covey says, "The key is not to prioritize my schedule, but to schedule my priorities." Stay in 'Quadrant 2' where first things are first, and not let the problems of others dictate your priorities. Say 'no' to the unimportant no matter how urgent, and 'yes' to the important.

William

Q. Tell me about an occasion when you felt really successful in managing your time.

I recall a recent situation where I was under tremendous pressure to produce a financial forecast for an upcoming board meeting. Since the company is relatively new (four years old) there is not a lot of solid history to rely upon for a forecast. The deadline was near and many other daily priorities need to be managed along the way... most of which were put on hold. One of the junior development specialists came to my office requesting assistance with writing and costing a proposal for a development project that would really stretch the expertise of the organization. The development group had never written a proposal for work of this nature. I recognized that my priority list was about to reshuffle. Normally, I would have requested the person come back at a later time when my current priority was completed, but I sensed an urgency and a valuable opportunity to assist - don't ask me why. I set aside my forecast priority and spent approximately three hours with this person teaching them about proposal writing and costing. It was the best three hours spent... for two reasons. One, the proposal writer was able to continue her work with knowledge of being 'on track' - she went away happy. The second reason, well, the break from preparing the forecast was necessary - but I didn't see it. At the time of the request for assistance, I didn't realize it, but I was so 'engulfed' in the forecast, that I was actually starting to 'spin my wheels.' After the three hour break I actually felt that the preparation of the forecast went smoother to a point that I completed it considerably sooner than expected. The proposal writer returned two days later to say that the client really liked the proposal and has requested more work at an additional cost. In other words the break was worth it. The moral of my story is not to be so rigid with the time management of the current task in hand that you lose sight of other priorities.

Q. *Tell me about some of your difficulties in time management.*

Time management is the most difficult when I am bombarded with constant interruptions by other staff. Even the simplest questions tend to break a focused concentration. This sometimes results in the 'reprioritizing' of my things-to-do lists because my focus has been momentarily diverted and embarrassingly enough, leads to some level of procrastination if the current task in hand is not high on my like-to-do list.

Q. *What advice can you offer to others of your type regarding time management?*

Try to maintain a short list of no more than three major priorities in your mind. This maintains some semblance of order in chaotic situations. It also helps you to prioritize on the run.

Try to maintain a written list of other priorities that do not need to be addressed immediately. Continue to add to the list during the day, then prioritize them at the end of the day when you can focus. This will help to shape the next day's workload. It also allows you time to sit down and think about possibly passing off some work to others or see links with other projects in hand. Dealing with priorities one at a time is not necessarily the best way to manage time. Sit back and look at your priorities from an eagle's perspective. A considerable amount of time can be managed properly through this process.

Discussion

As might be expected, ESTJ contributors tended to offer concrete details related to their style of time management. Being organized and getting things done was clearly important to them, but they had frustrations too.

Most of the ESTJ contributors were able to tell at least one time management success story. But they seemed prone to a common difficulty: interference in their plans, caused by unexpected situations or people with new ideas or questions.

This was not surprising. According to type theory, the force that animates ESTJs is the drive to run as much of the world as may be theirs to run. ESTJs are irresistibly drawn to structuring tasks so goals can be met. All this, for ESTJs, is the essence of living.

Since the challenge and excitement of getting each job done is such a driving force in their lives, it is hard for them to slow down the process by questioning the mission, studying the large picture, or communicating underlying motives to co-workers. Yet the neglect of these activities is frequently at the root of their frustrations.

When asked to provide suggestions for others like themselves, these ESTJs offered suggestions which would enable others like themselves to get their work done while preventing the frustration which, as one ESTJ put it, "flips my switch."

ESTJs were encouraged to be more aware of the big picture: "Sit back and look at your priorities from an eagle's perspective. A considerable amount of time can be managed properly through this process." "Look seriously at the changes or impact to your time; these may turn out to be a benefit rather than a reason to panic." One contributor told a story of how he personally made this discovery.

Since ESTJs like to focus on concrete objectives and the specific steps in getting there, most suggestions had to do with applying techniques and strategies which they found helpful in improving their own time management. "Make lists of tasks or things to do for the day." "Cross off the list when complete; this makes you feel good." "Put away things as soon as you are finished using them, so you don't lose time searching for anything."

Since ESTJs like to be in charge, working efficiently with others means communicating motives or instructions clearly, then "trying to get others to commit their part in front-end planning and follow-up work." When someone else is in charge or making a demand, ESTJs appreciate the same clear communication: "Try to get others to explain as clearly as possible what they want so that you can plan accordingly."

The need to prioritize was mentioned by several contributors. When the big picture is ignored, it is difficult to prioritize since everything can seem important. ESTJs were encouraged to take advice from Covey: "Don't prioritize your schedule; rather, schedule your priorities." Other suggestions had to do with specific techniques for keeping track of priorities: "Try to maintain a short list of no more than three major priorities in your mind..." "Try to maintain a written list of other priorities that do not need to be addressed immediately. Continue to add to the list during the day, then prioritize them at the end of the day when you can focus. This will help to shape the next day's workload..."

Clearly, most of the ESTJ contributors knew exactly the kind of suggestions people of their type would be likely to need and accept. They offered these suggestions in the matter-of-fact way which ESTJs prefer.

As mentioned earlier, type should not be an excuse for behaviour. Rather, an understanding of a person's natural preferences can be helpful in the development of an effective style which embraces whatever provides the driving force and gives life its meaning. The contributors offered some useful suggestions to help ESTJs reduce their stress while reaching their goals.

Helping ESTJs Find their Own Way

Characteristics and behaviours which could be expected of an ESTJ

- practical
- realistic
- want immediate, tangible and visible results
- enjoy getting things organized and done
- like to work in a stable and orderly environment
- expect goals to be achieved according to plan and on time
- attend to every detail
- give precise instructions
- value efficiency

- like things be done right the first time
- don't like to waste time questioning things which don't matter
- take work seriously
- have a strong sense of responsibility
- may take on too much
- don't like changes in plans
- like to set goals and make detailed plans
- work before play

Driving forces
To structure tasks so goals can be met.

Problems *most* likely to occur
Frustration with unexpected situations or interference in plans.

Solutions *least* likely to be followed
Slow down.

Suggestions

Here are some suggestions which will help you to be more productive.

1. Structure your work.

- Make lists of tasks or things to do for the day.
- Prioritize the list, most important things first, not a first-in and first-out approach.
- Cross off the list when complete; this makes you feel good.
- When you are working on several projects at the same time, integrate your lists if see to you can accomplish several tasks at the same time or setting, thus getting some synergy.
- Put away things as soon as you are finished using them, so you don't lose time searching for things.

2. Communicate effectively with others.

- Try to get others to commit their part in front-end planning and follow-up work.
- Try to get others to explain as clearly as possible what they want so that you can plan accordingly.

- Try to avoid having to make major changes by first getting feedback from the team to make sure everything can go according to plan
- Try to foster a supportive atmosphere among team members. Ask for help or offer help.

3. Be aware of the big picture.

- Dealing with priorities one at a time is not necessarily the best way to manage time. Sit back and look at your priorities from an 'eagle's perspective'.
- Get rid of the unnecessary. Concentrate on the important.
- Try to maintain a short list of no more than three major priorities in your mind. This provides some semblance of order in chaotic situations. It also helps you to prioritize on the run.
- Try to maintain a written list of other priorities that do not need to be addressed immediately. Continue to add to the list during the day, then prioritize them at the end of the day when you can focus. This will help to shape the next day's workload. It also allows you time to sit down and think about possibly passing off some work to others or see links with other projects in hand.
- Know the difference between the urgent and the important.

Chapter 8

ESTP

An Introduction to ESTP

If you are an ESTP, you are probably easy-going, adaptable and resourceful. You seem to do things in an effortless way, dealing confidently with most situations as they arise.

You enjoy life and people often find you fun to be with, but you can be tough when necessary. When problems arise, you have a realistic approach and like to take action. You can work well under pressure. You don't like things to be stalled by prolonged theoretical discussions that lead to nowhere.

You prefer to be free of routines and bureaucracy, and believe rules are meant to be broken if there is a better or easier way. You like variation and challenge in your work, but do not appreciate policy changes which do not make sense. If you work hard, you believe there should be some pay-off.

At work, you do not like to plan excessively. You organize as you go along and improvise if necessary. You have your own way of organizing things. This works for you, although other people may find your workstyle disturbing. Your easy-going style may cause others to think you are not taking your work seriously, and may be surprised when you actually produce excellent results. If something is important to you, you are more likely to ensure success by planning and organizing carefully.

I asked five ESTPs how they try to cope with time management. These ESTPs are not necessarily typical of their types, but their stories can provide helpful information for you and others. Several identify how they make the most of the strengths which result from their type preferences, and several tell how they compensate for their natural weaknesses. Some tell of difficulties yet unsolved. Together they provide some unique ideas and useful suggestions for ESTPs.

Stories, Ideas, & Suggestions

Charlie

Sharon, I would be glad to help, but with one preliminary comment. People tell me, and I would agree, that I work as an ESTJ type in some aspects of work when I know that ESTP will not work. For instance, when I know that ESTP methods will cause failure, I plan and prepare very carefully. I chair a committee that meets this Friday, and its job is very important to our School of Engineering and Technology. To insure success, I have prepared a manual of processes, history (committee is five years old), and resources.

On to your questions...

Q. *Tell me about an occasion when you felt really successful in managing your time.*

There was a time that I was teaching full time (I still am), doing research and conducting workshops with the MBTI, and developing software as a consultant. I was essentially doing three jobs at the same time. I was able to switch from the 'P' mode to the 'J' mode, I think because I learned to do that from early age, but also because all three areas of work were fun and enjoyable. I do not think I could have done it if I saw them as pure work for the sake of work.

Otherwise, I do not think in terms of time management. Perhaps time management is a conscious principle for 'J' type who might think in terms of schedules and managing time.

Q. *Tell me about some of your difficulties in time management.*

I try to do too much and overestimate how much I can do in a fixed time. I volunteer for a lot of non-required tasks because they sound like fun. (ESTJ gets in the way because I sometimes feel that no one can do it as well as I can). I often have to have a deadline in order to begin work. Otherwise, I find something more enjoyable to do. Luckily, I usually get things done before the deadline. I can think of only a few times that I did not, but we seem to be able to pick and choose which things will result in minor damage if they are not done. Usually, missing the deadline only hurts me, but I'm not sure that is true of other ESTPs. I imagine that some ESTPs would not care if missing a deadline hurts others. Once I set a deadline, though, I am very efficient. On the down side, things are done but not necessarily done very well because of working to a deadline.

Q. *What advice can you offer to others of your type regarding time management?*

1) If you put things off to the last minute, make sure that such actions do not cause others trouble in getting their work done.

2) Learn to say 'no' and do not volunteer for more than you can handle in the time you have available.

3) If you want to produce high quality work, give yourself plenty of time to refine your first pass at the project.

4) Learn to work in the 'J' mode for those occasions where early preparation is essential.

Q. *What help would you like to get regarding time management from others of your type?*

About the only thing I can think of at this time is help in overcoming crisis orientation, i.e., leaving things until the last minute. I know the theories, like setting goals, setting time lines, thinking about the people who need the results of my work, etc., but I still wait until the last minute.

Newman

I'll try to address your questions about time management, but I only have ten minutes.

Q. *Tell me about an occasion when you felt really successful in managing your time.*

As a general rule, I feel most successful about time management when I don't have too much on my schedule. I prefer to organize my days into blocks rather than hours or minutes. Thus I plan something for the

morning, afternoon, and evening. An example of a recent day when I felt
I managed my time well was the day I performed one lab assay in the
morning, worked out over lunch, performed another assay in the afternoon,
and met friends to watch a football game in the evening. That's my idea of
a pretty good day.

Q. Tell me about an occasion when you felt really successful in managing your time.

My difficulties in time management arise when I'm due at a certain place
at a specified time, especially if I have multiple commitments in a day.
I tend to run late for most classes and meetings. I do alright when I have
a bunch of appointments in a row, but if there is an hour or two in
between I start lagging again. I frequently forget morning appointments
because I keep my schedule, such as it is, on a computerized calendar
which I check in the morning when I get to work. Even if I check it in the
evening before leaving for the day, I often forget my schedule for the next
day unless there's something crucially important. And I don't find many
things crucially important.

Q. What advice can you offer to others of your type regarding time management?

My advice for time management for others of my type is to simply not over-
commit. Don't get trapped in a career or lifestyle which demands on-time
appearances and juggling of appointments. Simplify and be happy.

Q. What help would you like to get regarding time management from others of your type?

I have received all the help in the time management arena I wanted from
my ex-wife. She tried her darndest to get me to keep a pocket organizer
and to be more punctual. It didn't work, though I felt guilty more. I don't
think we ESTP's really care all that much about time management, and we
would prefer that the punctuality freaks get off our case.

My timer just went off. Okay, I admit it. I do use a timer when running my
science assays. If I didn't, I would forget I was running one and just leave
it half-done overnight. I hope this was helpful. Best wishes with your study.

Marie

I'd be happy to answer your questions re time management and being an ESTP (although sometimes I feel I'm more an ESFP):

Q. Tell me about an occasion when you felt really successful in managing your time.

I tend to get involved in a lot of activities, and thus overextend myself. For instance, I haven't been home in well over a week - I'm off attending various meetings, get togethers and visiting. I keep a daytimer mainly at work (I'd never look at it at home), where I write down all appointments and meetings, and to-do things, and some personal stuff. I find that I can group a lot of my errands into my work day (banking, grocery shopping, haircuts), although my natural tendency is to procrastinate! I also find if I make a personal commitment to someone, I am more likely to keep it more or less on track.

Q. Tell about some of your difficulties in time management.

I like to procrastinate. It's one of the things with which I am most efficient! I also try to do WAY TOO MUCH, and find that I'm so busy doing all sorts of stuff that nothing gets done at all. I do not like being pinned down to a schedule, either, which is really difficult since I am involved in so much stuff. I like doing, not planning. I take after my mother!

Q. What advice can you offer to others of your type regarding time management?

As much as I hate planning, I find I have to in order to be able to do the things I like. I don't think I'm an organized person by nature - I say I am 'J' so that I can be 'P'. Example - my kitchen cupboards/freezer/fridge are extremely tidy, and I don't collect clutter (if I do, it's organized clutter). I systematically get rid of things on a twice annual basis. I organize my stuff so that I can have time to be flexible. I have a girlfriend of mine who plans her life around cleaning her house, to the point where she won't go out "because it's Thursday night and I have to mop the floors." For me, I try to do little tasks in 15 minute bursts, so that I'll never miss doing something fun because I have no clean clothes to wear (which almost happened this weekend). Hope this helps.

Terri

Q. *Tell about an occasion when you felt really successful in managing your time.*

Not one occasion in particular. I enjoy having multiple projects on the go. When I can effectively meet deadlines, keep my paperwork organized, continue to meet and assist clients and run programs that meet community needs, I am happy.

Q. *Tell about some of your difficulties in time management.*

I have trouble prioritizing job tasks. Put off job duties that are tedious and then cram it all in the last minute. Enjoy high pressure and completing tasks on a tight schedule but don't give myself time to do a thorough job. Don't enjoy pushing paper which doesn't help the time management.

Q. *What advice can you offer to others of your type regarding time management?*

1. Be very organized.

2. Use time management tools to assist you: daytimer, project microsoft program.

3. Keep detailed notes, write everything down.

4. Keep a consistent schedule. I see clients three days a week at the same time. This consistency keeps me on the track and reliable.

5. Meet weekly for a meeting with co-workers to go over upcoming projects and tasks. This works as a reminder in case I have overlooked something.

Richard

A success: I could go to school for a week and not miss class from temptations... That's really good for me.

Difficulties: I'm sometimes led into temptations like making a promise and sometimes I have to break it. But I always try to keep my word.

Advice: Always keep your word and stay in your groove.

Discussion

It was hard to get responses from ESTPs because they do not like talking about time management. They are doers, not philosophizers; and they don't like the time management topic anyway, because they associate it with planning and they don't like planning. One person said: "Good luck getting your ESTP contributors, my boyfriend is a flaming ESTP and there's no way he'd do it." Another person said: "You're looking in the wrong place. They don't answer their e-mail regularly. Go to a pub and buy them a round and then they might answer your questions!" I wanted to be consistent and get all my responses on e-mail if possible so I did persevere. When I did finally get responses, I enjoyed their candour and cheerful self-acceptance.

Almost all of the ESTPs in this study were able to tell at least one successful time management story. But they seemed prone to a common difficulty: getting distracted.

This was not surprising. According to type theory, the force that animates ESTPs is the need to respond to current situations. ESTPs are irresistibly drawn to living in the moment. For ESTPs, this is an essential of living, although, being logical, they do recognize that some things have to be done. They prefer to deal with these problems as they arise.

Since responding to the moment and enjoying the present is such a driving force for their lives, ESTPs would be likely to rebel against advice which suggested that they plan carefully and stick with the plan. This would be an unacceptable way to live.

When asked to provide suggestions for others like themselves, these people offered suggestions which would enable ESTPs to get the essentials done and still have fun. They suggested: "Figure out ways to organize your stuff and do what you have to do so you won't miss the fun times." "Even if you hate planning, you may find you have to do a little planning in order to do the things you like." "Try working in 15 minute bursts, then do things you enjoy in between."

It's the things that happen spontaneously that make life worth living for ESTPs, so they want to leave room for that. "Don't over-commit." "Simplify your life and enjoy."

Although ESTPs prefer to use their logic over feeling, they do want to get along with other people. They can sometimes use this to help keep themselves on track: "If you put things off to the last minute, make sure that such actions do not cause others trouble in getting their work done." "Try meeting weekly with co-workers to go over upcoming projects and tasks. This works as a reminder in case you have overlooked something."

Logic can tell ESTPs that sometimes, if it is important to produce high quality work, they may have to do more planning than they would like. "If you want to produce high quality work, give yourself plenty of time to refine your first pass at the project." "Learn to work in the 'J' mode for those occasions where early preparation is essential." "Use time management tools to assist you even if you hate pushing paper." "Try keeping a consistent schedule..."

As mentioned earlier, type should not be an excuse for behaviour. Rather, an understanding of a person's natural preferences can be helpful in the development of an effective style which embraces whatever provides the driving force and gives life its meaning. The contributors offered some useful suggestions to help ESTPs to be more effective time managers while still being themselves.

Helping ESTPs Find their Own Way

Characteristics and behaviours which could be expected of an ESTP

- easy-going
- adaptable
- resourceful
- seem to do things in an effortless way
- deal confidently with most situations as they arise
- enjoy life
- fun to be with
- tough when necessary
- like to take action
- work well under pressure
- not much interested in theory
- prefer to be free of routines and bureaucracy
- like variation
- believe there should be some pay-off for working hard
- organize along the way
- improvise when necessary
- have own way of organizing things
- can plan carefully if something is important

Driving forces
Enjoying the moment, dealing with problems as they arise.

Problems *most* likely to occur
Rely too much on improvising, sometimes causing undue pressure.

Solutions *least* likely to be followed
Always plan ahead.

Suggestions

Here are some suggestions to help you get the essentials done and still have fun.

1. Free yourself up to do what you like.
- Even if you hate planning, you may find you have to do a little planning in order to do the things you like.
- Figure out ways to organize your stuff and do what you have to do so you won't miss out on the fun times.

2. Know your time limitations.
- Don't over-commit: Learn to say 'no' and do not volunteer for more than you can handle in the time you have available.
- If you want to produce high quality work, give yourself plenty to time to refine your first pass at the project.
- Simplify your life and enjoy.

3. Know your own workstyle.
- If you tend to put things off to the last minute, make sure that such actions do not cause others trouble in getting their work done.
- Try working in 15 minute bursts, then do things you enjoy in between.

4. Learn some tricks from organized people to help you get your work done, especially if it is very important.
- Use time management tools to assist you: e.g. daytimer - even if you hate pushing paper!
- Try keeping a consistent schedule. The consistency will keep you on track and reliable.
- Try meeting weekly with co-workers to go over upcoming projects and tasks. This works as a reminder in case you have overlooked something.

5. Consider alternatives.
- Don't get trapped in a career or lifestyle which demands on-time appearances and juggling of appointments.

Chapter 9

INFJ

An Introduction to INFJ

If you are an INFJ, you are likely to be a person with a strong inner vision who values harmony and good fellowship. You are likely to make contributions which improve human welfare.

You recognize that rules, systems, and procedures can help people to function effectively but you would implement these cautiously to avoid interfering in human freedom and autonomy. You believe changes should be implemented with care, and that the most meaningful and lasting changes are those which evolve over time. You believe that the purpose of the organization needs to be accomplished, but not at the expense of the needs of the people involved.

You approach your work seriously and often produce more than is expected, especially if you understand and value the underlying purpose of the job. You naturally provide others with encouragement and support, and appreciate the same for yourself.

You like a pleasant workplace where you have an opportunity to approach challenging and creative projects. Your workstyle is generally well organized. It is important for you to be able to complete what you do.

Sometimes your work may consume so much time and energy that your own needs are neglected. You can feel overwhelmed if you are interrupted by too many simultaneous or conflicting demands. Furthermore, dealing with the needs of other people, however important this may be, can delay the completion of your work.

I asked six INFJs how they try to cope with time management. These INFJs are not necessarily typical of their types, but their stories can provide helpful information for you and others. Several identify how they make the most of the strengths which result from their type preferences, and several tell how they compensate for their natural weaknesses. Some tell of difficulties yet unsolved. Together they provide some unique ideas and useful suggestions for INFJs.

Stories, Ideas, & Suggestions

Karen

Sorry, it's taken so long to reply.

Q. *Tell me about an occasion when you felt really successful in managing your time.*

A time where I felt really successful in time management was when I was working full-time, enrolled in a week-end college program working on my bachelor's degree, enrolled at the community college to pick up an additional fourth class, all while caring for a family (husband and three small children at the time). I look back on it and wonder how I did it. According to my husband, he didn't suffer. According to my children, they did not suffer. I was tired but focused and did graduate.

Q. *Tell me about some of your difficulties in time management.*

Difficulties can arise for a number of reasons: putting off scheduling a doctor's appointment (fear of the unknown); putting off the dentist appointment (fear of pain); putting off having to deal with issues that are sensitive or potentially emotional for me (as a manager having to deal with an employee, that I like, not meeting performance expectations). Perhaps, the latter is due to the 'F'. My shortcomings with time management seem to center on the initiation of things I don't want to do. But once I get going, I'm o.k. and on top of things.

I don't know that anyone can help me with the doctor or dentist (smile). But any suggestions that might increase my comfort level with the last example would be helpful.

Advice for other INFJs:

Be true to yourself. First, you must know who you are. Second, accept who you are (the good and not so good) Third, genuinely like who you are. Why? Because just as it has been said that you can tell what one's values are by looking at their chequebook register; you want to know that your time is being spent on those activities or with those people that you deem important, near and dear to your heart, in concert with your personal values. So, values clarification is a good exercise. I absolutely love self-assessments where I put together my own plan of action based on any identified gaps between what's going on today and what I want or where I want to be.

The serenity prayer is helpful. Again, with a solid foundation in values, I maintain my own sense of sanity during the chaos of trying to be all things to all people. I had to learn to stop beating up on myself for not being 'superwoman'. I am also a Covey advocate and believe that I am the owner of how I choose to respond to a given situation.

I hope this is helpful stuff.

Eduardo

I'll be glad to answer your questions...

Q. Tell me about an occasion when you felt really successful in managing your time.

Success in time management comes about in general when I succeed in making up a list of what I have to do and I find that I have been able to do it in the time I have allotted to the planned activities. I experience time as structures that you fill in but these structures are always on the move. I find myself having an approximate guess at the time it is at a given moment without looking at the watch. Looking at the watch is rather a way of verifying if I'm right in my guessing. When I guess right I feel successful because somehow I have the impression that I have been going with the flow and therefore carrying out the planned activities. Another good feeling comes about when I don't try to control or 'manage' time but rather when I perceive that time has a rhythm of its own and events are 'happenings' or coincidences that click with my own fluid inner state of mind. Examples of the two kinds of perception that provoke a feeling of success are numerous. Rather than specific instances, what I have described is a habitual tendency.

Q. *Tell me about some of your difficulties in time management.*

The most unsuccessful experiences of time management are related to: being late, not meeting deadlines, putting things off, not finishing something that I started, and in general not giving closure to things. On the other hand, I feel that I have not been successful if my plans are too ambitious for the time available. This last instance is doubly painful because pushing myself unrealistically results in failure of closure, and at the same time, I have been forcing the beautiful balance of the outer world.

Q. *What advice can you offer to others of your type regarding time management?*

Try to be aware of your personal balance between the time you spend in introverted activities and the time spent in extraverted activities. Don't overdo it in one sense or the other. Since these two attitudes are always in dynamic interplay one can easily exaggerate and behave either in an absent-minded or distracted way (introverted 'N') or become exhausted in too much personal interaction (extraverted 'F'). This is important for the planning aspect of time management. Since our intuition can provide us with beautiful and important goals and objectives which we try to implement, we have a tendency to disregard details and sometimes we may overlook realistic aspects of the situation and force closure ahead of time. We may have to become aware of the need to be flexible and accommodating with our time by appreciating the 'P' approach.

Mary

Q. *Tell me about an occasion when you felt really successful in managing your time.*

I wrote a Ph.D. dissertation while working full-time and raising two kids (I had completed the course work and qualifying exams, and had my proposal accepted just before taking the full-time job). I managed to do this by using a principle from a time management course on 'managing by objectives.' Essentially, I sketched out an overview, segments, and how the segments tied together. I was able to take a folder in to work relating to any given segment and write during my lunch hour (brought my own lunch); I also wrote all day every other Sunday while my kids were at their Dad's. It took a year.

Q. *What are some of your difficulties in time management?*

These almost invariably relate to letting myself get overwhelmed and/or anxious about how I'm going to get it all done. But I always pull through at the last minute. In fact, I often do a better job that way because I know there's no time left and I push through my anxiety into a fairly creative place.

Q. *What advice can you offer others of your type?*

Be clear about your objectives, and particularly what purpose you have in setting this goal; chunk it down to manageable pieces without losing sight of the overall picture; trust your intuition; don't let yourself get pulled off course too much by others' needs.

Q. *What help would you like to get regarding time management from others of your type?*

Not sure. I'm fairly advanced in years and feel I've wrestled this issue to the ground (lots of others to work on), but I'd love to see what you come up with.

Good luck. Let me know if you need anything further.

Wayne

Here are my first thoughts related to your research on time management styles and MBTI types. When I have an opportunity, I'll write more.

My education, early career, and experiences were highly 'ST': very detailed, complete with schedules, specific targets, measurements, and deadlines. I became strong with numbers and detailed planning; I even managed an accounting department for four years while on my first job. In those days I had not learned about MBTI yet so I couldn't understand why I never felt satisfied for very long with achieving specific goals. I knew that there had to be something else for me, something that would possibly be just over the next hill. I recognized that I was happiest when I first took on a new project or job. I also figured out that once I became familiar with any subject to the point that I understood it and could anticipate the results, I soon became bored... ready for a new challenge.

I was an athlete with a strong drive to be the best in all sports. Although being the best was not always the case, athletics instilled in me a discipline to work hard and a mental toughness to push myself to identify my weaknesses and to build upon my strengths. I was taught to 'never give up!' In fact, I was able to attend a good college because I could play football and baseball well. My five years there were on athletic scholarships in both sports. But even then, I felt there had to be something more than I was experiencing. I could 'see' and 'feel' things that others never seemed to experience. I just thought I was different, and, of course, I couldn't explain what it was... I couldn't even understand it myself. I know now that I was an INFJ in an 'ST' world.

In college and in the early years of my work career I could easily and quickly grasp the big picture, but I didn't like spending hours (sometimes days and days) on the details that 'anyone could do.' However, I quickly learned that to be successful in the business world I also had to do all of the details, and do them on time. Timing is an important issue in a highly competitive environment.

While I was with my first company (a large industrial firm), I learned critical-path planning for project management. PERT charts, schedules, materials, manpower, and dollars were the elements we managed, all having to come together in a coordinated, timely fashion. Details, details, details!

Time management was something I learned to be good at because I knew I had to have that discipline to be 'successful.' Again, it wasn't until I started learning about MBTI and the various preferences of people that I began to understand what I was experiencing on the inside and why I had never been satisfied for very long. Of course, MBTI does not answer all of the questions, but it helped me to recognize who I was and why I felt the way I did. In addition, I have a very strong value system that guides my decisions and actions (though certainly not always perfectly).

Q. Tell me about an occasion when you felt really successful in managing your time.

Time management for me today has changed from what it was early in my career. Today I first define what is truly important and what is not. I try to establish priorities, both short-term as well as long-range. And although I can't always work on the most important items first, I'm getting better at it. Fortunately, I'm in a position now in which I can surround myself with people who have strengths and desires to work on things I'd rather not. I'm better at strategic planning (seeing around corners), anticipating trends and results, and working with the people issues. My management style is that of a coach and mentor. My bosses, the chairman and the board of directors, are all 'STs' who speak 'finances.' I can do that too, but I prefer the big picture stuff and the people relationships. I personally conduct a lot of our training also... but I get others to handle the schedules and the specifics of who, what, when, where, etc.

Q. Tell me about some of your difficulties in time management.

The thing that can still cause a problem for me is my tendency to work in spurts of energy. I may let details go until the last minute, then work like crazy to get it done. I'm o.k. with that because I know how I am, but I can drive our engineers and accountants up the wall. Of course they want everything laid out in the smallest detail weeks ahead of time! Good teamwork requires me to communicate long before our targeted dates what I see and feel so others can fill in the gaps as well as test my vision. I may fire retro-rockets for course corrections throughout the days, weeks, or months... no problem. On occasions I get details that show me that my original intuitions were not entirely accurate, so we make mid-course corrections.

Q. What advice can you offer to others of your type regarding time management?

I believe that the key words are DISCIPLINE and BALANCE. We need discipline to do certain tasks even though we may not be entirely comfortable with them. We need to achieve balance by developing our auxiliary and least preferred functions. I'm glad that my education and early career experiences forced me to develop my 'back-up' systems to the degree they are today. Now I can use and further develop my 'NF' preferences which are natural for me. I realize this approach may not fit everyone, especially those who have no interest in the business world. But I do feel that many 'NFs' struggle with time management because they lack the mental discipline and the balance of functions to consciously choose and use the function(s) most appropriate for the situation. I'm not comfortable with people saying, "well, I can't do that because it's just not me."

I like what Steven Covey says about time management in his book: *First Things First'* (paraphrased): "What if we work on climbing the ladder of success for years only to find out that it was leaning against the wrong wall?" I use a Franklin planner to schedule the details of my daily life and to handle the needs of others who require a lot of structure. My secretary/ administrative assistant is very detailed and organized. We share a similar value system and a concern for other people. I don't impose my preferences on others, in fact, we all discuss each other's preferences and strengths, then work to openly complement each other. (We seem to minimize the ego problems because there is a good level of mutual trust). I have an excellent follow-up system that my assistant administers for me. The things I must do today are always in front of me. The things I don't need to spend time on today are in our system to 'pop-out' at the appropriate time. My desk is usually clean except for the items I'm working on. We 'plan our work and work our plan.' I find that by assigning priorities first, I usually have time to work on what's truly important.

I wonder sometimes why it's difficult for some people to recognize that they can accomplish more (especially more important things) by first defining what's really important, then allowing other people to take on pieces that better fit their capabilities or preferences. My time management is much better when I help people develop their capabilities and thus take on more and more important assignments. The more I help them grow, the more time I have to do what I like best...

Our managers are mostly engineers. I'm not an engineer so I don't try to do what they do technically. And they have learned to come to me to help them look at the big picture or to guide them in their dealings with people issues. That's not to say that everything always runs smoothly, it does not. But I have confidence that we will usually determine the root-cause of problems, then assign the appropriate people to solve the problem... not just the symptoms. When we solve the true problems, we free up even more time.

I have a philosophy I call 'planned neglect.' If it's not truly important for me to work on at the moment, I put it aside. It will go in my follow-up system if I keep it at all, to be considered later if it merits my time.

Paul

Some brief responses to your questions:

Q. Tell me about an occasion when you felt really successful in managing your time.

Generally I manage time well and in an earlier job when I was developing an extensive adventure camping programme for young people it became a matter for humour that I would turn up on a given spot in the mountains within seconds of when I said I would be there. I was not at all conscious of taking strategic action to ensure that. So it is not easy for me to identify a time when I manage time really well. I think for me to manage time well means letting go of a projected deadline for accomplishing a set number of tasks and letting things run outside time. That is the opposite to my compulsion. So I generally accomplish tasks within the time frame allocated. Much to the frustration of some people around me.

One strength I have is that tasks are done as they arrive so I do not need to have strategies in place for making sure I remember them at a later time. I usually answer e-mail the day it comes. If I delay it any longer I would have to have a system, to make sure I remembered it or to decide not to respond.

Ann

Hello!

I've been thinking about it for the past few days, and there aren't really any specific occasions when I felt successful in managing my time. I guess this past summer term would count because I was on such a strict schedule between classes and work. I would get up in time to go to class at 9:15, and after it got out at 10:45, I would go and check my e-mail till 11:00. Then I would go back to my room to read (I took British Literature and Western Civ I, so I had a lot of reading to do), or, more often, sleep. I would meet my boyfriend for lunch at 12:30, and we would go to class at 1:15. I went to work straight after class and usually worked from 3:00 to 6:00 at a Hallmark store. Then I would return to my dorm room, eat dinner, and study until I went to bed around 11:00. This was my normal routine for school nights, and weekends were generally a bit freer. I did manage to make it through the summer term with my sanity and with A's in both courses. That's the best time-management I've done so far.

Q. Tell me about some of your difficulties in time management.

I'm really good at setting a schedule, but I'm easily distracted from it by my boyfriend, the internet, and television. Also, sometimes I get so burned out on the schedule that it goes 'kaput' for a few days.

Q. What advice can you offer to others of your type regarding time management?

Set a schedule but realize that it's not written in stone, get plenty of rest, and always schedule 'me' time to be alone and do stuff that you really enjoy.

Q. What help would you like to get regarding time management from others of your type?

How do I know when I'm doing too much? That's the only problem with mine.

Discussion

Although almost all of the INFJ contributors were able to tell at least one time management success story, some seemed to feel overloaded and stressed at times.

This is not surprising. According to type theory, the force that animates INFJs is the vision of inner-driven possibilities. They are future oriented, directing their insight and inspiration toward an understanding of themselves and the human condition. They have a deep desire to follow through but they are also strongly influenced by their feeling auxiliary which means they feel they must consider the human side of things. It is difficult to keep these two forces in balance.

Since accomplishing their own plans without sacrificing human values is so important in their lives, it is understandable that some of them would feel overburdened and stressed. It is a heavy load to be constantly questioning objectives and weighing alternatives in light of your values and the values of those around you. When asked to provide suggestions for others like themselves, these INFJs seemed to be looking for ways to help ensure that the objectives were good before expending too much time. "You want to know that your time is being spent on those activities or with those people that you deem important, near and dear to your heart, in concert with your personal values... Do a self-assessment where you put together your own plan of action based on any identified gaps between what's going on today and what you want or where you want to be." "Be clear about your objectives and particularly what purpose you have in setting this goal."

Since achieving the right purposes in terms of human implications is so important to INFJs, prioritizing is an important part of the time management process for them. "Prioritize by finding out 'why' does this need to be done by then, or at all, and what will happen if it is not."

Attention to human needs often results in distractions. Some suggestions focused on ensuring that these distractions do not interfere in the ultimate purpose of the project. "Don't let yourself get pulled off course too much by others' needs." At the same time, it is important for the INFJ to at least consider the human need which has emerged. "Set a schedule but realize that it's not written in stone."

Since it can be so time consuming, confusing, and exhausting to be constantly questioning objectives, weighing alternatives, prioritizing goals and considering arising needs, some suggestions attempted to deal with the resulting stress and fatigue. "Get plenty of rest." "Always schedule 'me' time to be alone and do stuff you really enjoy." "Chunk your work down to manageable pieces without losing sight of the overall picture." "Accept who you are (the good and not so good)." "Use the serenity prayer." "Try to be aware of the personal balance between introverted and extraverted activities. Don't overlook either."

There was also some practical advice for getting the job completed. "Work on discipline and balance (to do certain tasks even though you are not entirely comfortable with them)." "If possible, surround yourself with people who like to do the kinds of things you don't like to do." "...Determine the root-cause of problems and then assign the appropriate people to solve the problems." "Try not to overlook the realistic aspects of the activity."

As mentioned earlier, type should not be an excuse for behaviour. Rather, an understanding of a person's natural preferences can be helpful in the development of an effective style which embraces whatever provides the driving force and gives life its meaning. The contributors offered some useful suggestions to help INFJs deal with the conflict between the desire to make closure and the desire to meet the ideals and needs of the people involved.

Helping INFJs Find their Own Way

Characteristics and behaviours which could be expected of an INFJ

- have a strong inner vision
- values harmony in relationships
- concerned with human welfare
- do not want rules and systems to interfere with human needs
- believe changes should be implemented with care
- approach work seriously

- often produce more than is expected
- naturally provide others with encouragement and support
- workstyle generally well organized
- want to complete tasks
- sometimes neglect own needs
- can feel overwhelmed by too many simultaneous or conflicting demands

Driving forces
Deep desire to act on values and ideals, especially with regard to the human condition.

Problems *most* likely to occur
Conflict between desire to make closure and desire to meet ideals and needs of the people involved.

Solutions *least* likely to be followed
Stop questioning so much, just get the job done.

Suggestions

Here are some suggestions which may help you to plan your work and life in a balanced way.

1. Take time to reflect on the meaning of your work.
- Be true to yourself:
  1) Know who you are.
  2) Accept who you are (the good and not so good)
  3) Genuinely like who you are.
  You want to know that your time is being spent on those activities or with those people that you deem important, near and dear to your heart, in concert with your personal values.
- Define what is truly important and what is not.
- Do a self-assessment where you put together your own plan of action based on any identified gaps between what's going on today and what you want or where you want to be.
- Prioritize by finding out 'why' does this need to be done by then, or at all, and what will happen if it is not.
- Be clear about your objectives, and particularly what purpose you have in setting this goal.
- Establish priorities, both short-time and long-range. Try to work on the most important things first.

2. Keep your focus.
- Set a schedule but realize that it's not written in stone.
- Chunk your work down to management pieces without losing sight of the overall picture.
- Don't let yourself get pulled off course too much by others' needs.
- Work on discipline (to do certain tasks even though you are not entirely comfortable with them).

3. Delegate if you can.
- If possible, surround yourself with people who like to do the kinds of things you don't like to do.
- Remember that if you determine the root-cause of problems and then assign the appropriate people to solve the problems (not just treat the systems) you will solve the true problems and eventually free up more time.

4. Look after yourself.
- Get plenty or rest.
- Always schedule 'me' time to be alone and do stuff you really enjoy.
- Use the serenity prayer.

Chapter 10

INFP

An Introduction to INFP

If you are an INFP, you are probably are at your best in individual work involving personal values. You have a strong sense of duty and are faithful to purposes, people and causes which you truly care about.

You appreciate an environment which encourages harmony, mutual support and cooperation. Although you value relationships, you can work well alone, using the solitude for contemplation. Where the objectives are something you care deeply about, you can become totally absorbed in a project.

With your vision and consideration of human values, you have the potential to make important long-lasting contributions. But when you become immersed in a project, time disappears. In your heart you do not want to 'manage' time, because time is life to be lived in and appreciated, not commodified, chunked or linearized. What is important is to make a contribution and to do it well.

Your innate desire to 'do it well' - to meet your highest ideals when the project is one you care deeply about - further robs you of time, because you may find yourself 'perfecting' on and on. Understanding that projects can become totally absorbing for you can cause you to postpone getting started... the feeling that "I don't want to go there yet."

When you are absorbed in a meaningful project, you can become so immersed that everyday tasks have less importance to you. This may cause you to neglect things or lose things and may make you seem disorganized to others and even to yourself - yet you know that you do have a clear sense of purpose and an emerging creative design. You sense that traditional styles of organization with rigid rules or structures would be unhelpful or even counterproductive to your overall purpose.

I asked five INFPs how they try to cope with such issues. These INFPs are not necessarily typical of their types, but their stories can provide helpful insights and ideas for you and others. Several identify how they make the most of the strengths which result from their type preferences, and several tell how they compensate for their natural weaknesses. Some tell of difficulties yet unsolved. Together they provide some unique ideas and useful suggestions for INFPs.

Stories, Ideas, & Suggestions

Sarah

Q. Tell me about an occasion when you felt really successful in managing your time.

This is a rare experience. Success in time management is something I feel when I manage to get to places on time and leave tasks on time to engage in the next one. Generally, this seems to me to be related to being in a certain mood/attitude: when I am not overly perfectionistic and self-critical, and feeling kind of relaxed, I am more likely to not perseverate or obsess— the things that lead me to stay too long with one task and not allow enough time for the next one. I think I also do this best when I break up the tasks to be small enough so that they are really 'doable' in the specific time frame I plot out — my time management thrives only if I have a sense of success and completion with small tasks throughout the day.

Q. Tell me about some of your difficulties in time management.

I have struggled a lot with getting things done in advance, rather than being inspired and creative at the last minute. One of my difficulties is that SOMETIMES when I do manage to prepare in advance, I actually don't have the sparkle or creative energy to make the work good—especially if we are talking about a public presentation. Also, I am easily distracted by the needs of others, and in general I say 'yes' to too many requests, which interfere with my own private preparation time. My own time doesn't seem like 'real work' to me, even though it is absolutely necessary for what I must produce. I tend to count 'real work' as those things that involve face to face contact with people, and this approach is counterproductive, because face to face contact with people tends to exhaust, rather than recharge me.

Q. What advice can you offer to others of your type regarding time management?

Remember that solitude working time is real work as much as performance and social interaction is. Make tasks very small and practice being realistic in estimating how much time it will take to do things. Overestimate the time needed.

Q. What help would you like to get regarding time management from others of your type?

Just more information on strategies people have tried, and what has worked. How time management and self-esteem can be related. How to deal with the fatigue that comes over me sometimes when I have been 'people pleasing' for too long and need to recharge my batteries.

Hope that helps.

David

By and large time management is not an issue for me. I get done what I need to get done and the things I don't do are a function of how important they are and how much time I have and whether other people are involved. I do get my agendas completed fairly expeditiously.

So in terms of your research I don't know what else I can say. If you need more ask me again.

Pat

Procrastination is a problem I have to actively deal with by forcing myself to begin. But once I begin, a project takes on a life of its own, just that beginning a big task is not always easy. When I am involved, it is hard for me to put things down. Feel a strong sense of responsibility about getting things done as projected.

I am interested in your responses, actually for all types. I am a handwriting analyst and so think about how different personality types use their energy (and time being part of that) all the time. Keep me informed of your results please.

Sherril

No time to respond! Hope it's not too late. Anyway, here are some Sunday morning musings. Good luck with your research. Would be very interested in your results for my type.

Seriously, this INFP is a full-time employed person, spouse and mother, and full-time Master's student. I am peaking now in terms of my work on Master's project (in Human Systems Intervention) and expect to finish my project within the next three weeks and then begin writing up the dissertation, which will take me into January, I expect.

I always have several projects going on at one time. I pick and choose these projects and am usually quite able to say no if I feel I cannot give my all to it. I like to have a busy life, but it is also VERY important for me to schedule times for solitude and reflection. Some of my favourite times are when my family is out of the house and I hop into bed with my journal and a dozen books beside me. This is how I am able to balance things and be good to myself.

I haven't really thought much about 'time management' per se; I have priorities, which shift constantly, and I just structure my days so that I can meet them. It frustrates me when I cannot give my full, mindful attention to something important, so I really have learned to pick and choose my activities carefully, leaving enough space for family, fun learning, work and alone-time.

I guess you can figure out from my delayed response that this wasn't a top priority for me - I do apologize for that - nevertheless, I want to thank you for including me in your request.

Again, best of luck!

Jan

I hope it is not too late... as an INFP — besides the normal procrastination — we don't really like to answer these honestly, because it points out our weak spots! But I will (answer honestly)... not to worry!

Q. *Tell me about an occasion when you felt really successful in managing your time.*

In graduate school. I went back to an Executive MBA program... so I was working full time and going to school full time. I had very little free time. My life was so full and so scheduled that I was able to get an incredible amount done in a very structured way...

Q. *Tell me about some of your difficulties in time management*

The very topic is difficult.

Because work naturally emerges and it isn't 'right' or 'good enough' or 'resolved' until it is... this can take a long time. So, the pressure of a deadline helps to get started but not necessarily to finish... because it has to be 'just right.'

I like to be spontaneous and work at my own pace and so to structure things can be annoying. Also, things change constantly, so time management — the schedule has to be flexible enough to constantly change it.

Q. *What advice can you offer to others of your type regarding time management?*

Hmmm... This is what I do...

If I can't do everything, I stop and prioritize the areas of importance. I spend some time planning how it will be done. Then I will proceed with the most important items/areas first. If critical, I will allocate a certain amount of time for each task or area. I do this only when it is critical or else it would cause too much stress and not be good.

Typically, I try to set my life up so that I don't have to do the 'structured' form of time management (i.e., the Covey/Franklin style, etc.). I typically will have big picture ideas of what needs to be done over the next months/ half year/year... and work towards those... The description in the paragraph above is when things are so tight that I need to add formal structure.

On the other hand, there is a downside to the big picture time management. The positive is that it is more balanced for me (mind, body, emotion, spirit). The downside is that not as much gets done — and I often will feel that I am not doing enough.

Oh... I would also recommend taking the Covey/Franklin style time management courses or do the reading — so that you have the knowledge of the concepts, etc. There may be parts of those programs that are helpful for you, even if the whole system is not.

Q. *What help would you like to get regarding time management from others of your type?*

Hmmm... I would love to know how others do it... because it is a constant struggle. It is that trade off between being who we are and what the world is. If there is a way to mesh the two gracefully — fantastic! So, I am very open to ideas on time management for 'NFPs.'

In reality... and somewhat jokingly, I need a keeper. I hope this helps... if you want more detail... let me know... I am happy to provide it.

Best regards.

Discussion

Most of the INFP contributors were able to tell at least one time management success story. But almost all seemed prone to fatigue caused by the effort to live their own high ideals both in their relationships with others and with the project which absorbs their attention.

This was not surprising. According to type theory, the force that animates INFPs is the desire for harmony in the inner world of feeling. INFPs deeply need to feel that their ideals are being lived in everything they do, so they must be constantly aware of emerging feelings and needs. This is exhausting and time consuming. Yet, for INFPs, this is the essence of living.

The creative project requires total absorption, but at the same time, the needs of people (especially those in the inner circle) must be met. To suggest that INFPs use a logical approach to structure their lives may seem in complete opposition to the openness that is required.

The contributors to this study seemed to understand this. When asked to provide suggestions for others like themselves, they offered ideas which would enable INFPs to do their work in their own way, while not draining their energy completely.

Since INFPs know that serving their ideals is always going to be important, the best thing to do is to try to make enough space in their lives so that their ideals can be well served. "Try to balance things (mind, body, emotion, spirit), and try not to feel guilty if this means getting less done." "Leave space for family, fun learning, work and alone-time." "Pick and choose activities carefully so that you can give your full mindful attention on what you do." "Overestimate the time needed." "Schedule time for solitude and reflection." "Find ways to get away from 'people pleasing' for a while so you can fight fatigue and recharge your batteries." "Remember that solitude working time is as important as social interaction."

Some contributors recognized that some structure might be necessary. "Try to set things up so that you don't have to structure your time too tightly. But you can do it if you have to..." as Sherril points out, especially if you are the one doing the structuring! "Divide projects into small tasks" (without losing sight of the big picture, which is so important). "Look at the time available and the people involved and do what has to be done." "Practice being realistic in estimating how much time is will take to do things." "Consider taking the Covey/Franklin style time management courses or do the reading... there may be parts of those programs that are helpful for you even if the whole system is not." The latter suggestion was made gently, in the hopes of not offending INFP sensitivities. Even so, when INFPs were asked to consider this suggestion, several didn't like it.

As mentioned earlier, type should not be an excuse for behaviour. Rather, an understanding of a person's natural preferences can be helpful in the development of an effective style which embraces whatever provides the driving force and gives life its joy and meaning. The contributors, by recognizing what is important in their own lives, were able to offer some useful ideas for INFPs.

Helping INFPs Find their Own Way

Characteristics and behaviours which could be expected of an INFP

- best in individual work involving personal values

- faithful to obligations, purposes, people and causes which they truly care about

- appreciate an environment which encourages harmony

- like people to work in a spirit of mutual support and cooperation

- use solitude for contemplation

- can become totally absorbed in a project

- do not want to 'manage' time because time is life to be lived in and appreciated

- want to make a contribution and to do it well

- when involved in a meaningful project, everyday tasks have less importance

Driving forces
The desire for harmony in the inner world of feeling.

Problems *most* likely to occur
Fatigue, from the effort of trying to always reach their ideals.

Solutions *least* likely to be followed
Use someone else's structure.

Suggestions

Here are some suggestions which will enable you to work in your own way.

1. Make enough space in your life so that your ideals can be well served.

- Try to balance things (mind, body, emotion, spirit), and try not to feel guilty if this means getting less done.
- Leave space for family, fun learning, work and alone-time.
- Pick and choose activities carefully so you can give your full mindful attention on what you do.

2. Find ways to recharge your energy.

- Schedule time for solitude and reflection.
- Remember that solitude working time is as important as social interaction.
- Find ways to get away from 'people pleasing' for a while so you can fight fatigue and recharge your batteries.

3. Remember that reaching your ideals takes more time.

- Practice being realistic in estimating how much time it will take to do things.
- Keep a clear sense of priorities. Look at the time available and the people involved and do what has to be done.
- Divide projects into small tasks.
- Overestimate the time needed.
- Try to set things up so that you don't have to structure your time too tightly. But you can do it if you must.

Chapter 11

INTJ

An Introduction to INTJ

If you are an INTJ, you are probably an intensely individualistic person. You are more interested in pioneering new pathways than in following old routines. You have tremendous drive and determination.

Your workstyle probably involves developing long-range goals and structuring step-by-step implementation which takes into account the efficient and effective use of resources. You work well autonomously and independently, and often approach objectives with single-minded intensity. When communicating with others you appreciate precision; when working together you expect efficiency. You have high standards for achievement for yourself and others, and as a result, you may push yourself and others, and perhaps lose patience with those who are less competent or efficient than yourself.

You are likely to be a master at developing strategies and models. You are probably excellent at organizing procedures and strategies to achieve your goals. With your natural inclination for developing structure and your drive to achieve objectives, it is unlikely that you have time management problems. However, your tendency to set ever-higher standards may cause you to consider time management issues as part of your strategic planning process.

As I was recruiting participants for my study, I noticed that the INTJs responded promptly, and were precise and succinct in their answers. Although no one had severe time management problems, several were open to finding ways to improve.

What follows are responses from the first six INTJs who responded to my e-mail request. These INTJs are not necessarily typical of their types, but their responses can provide helpful insights and ideas. Several identify how they make the most of the strengths which result from their type preferences. Together they provide some unique ideas and useful suggestions for INTJs.

Stories, Ideas, & Suggestions

Mohan

Success with managing time:

I feel successful when I am in a position to manage the routine tasks and ensure that they happen. The tasks/activities which are important to me get priority. I tend to get lost when there are too many routine things to be done. When I manage these, I feel that I have managed my time.

Difficulties in managing time:

a) Dealing with interrupts.

b) Tend to procrastinate when I do not see the task adding any value.

Advice to others of the same type:

I have found that checklists work very well for me (for the routine tasks). I use these to ensure that the routine tasks get completed. There is a sense of relief when I complete the tasks listed. I had mentioned above that the ones important to me get done. The difficulty I have is with tasks which need to be done but are neither important to me nor do they seem interesting. The checklists help me focus on these and I tend to complete them as quickly as possible. This gives me ample time to spend on my areas of interest.

I do not use checklists in areas which are of interest to me; out here I tend to go along with the flow and find this interesting.

Help that I would like:

a) How do other INTJs manage interrupts?

b) How do they deal with procrastination?

Lynn

Q. Tell me about an occasion when you felt really successful in managing your time.

I almost always feel successful at managing my time. It has always come very easily to me. A year ago I started a new job as a half-time associate pastor in a thriving congregation. There is plenty more work to do than there is time to do it. Over the course of the year I have tracked my hours and in general I have kept them around 25 hours per week, which was my goal. I have observed the kinds of things I need to say 'no' to in order to manage my time. Sometimes I take on more than 25 hours worth, but I make the conscious decision to do so.

Q. Tell me about some of your difficulties in time management.

Once this year several things fell in my lap because of circumstances beyond my control. For a couple of weeks I had way too much work to do. It took me a couple of weeks to figure out what to delegate and to get my head above water. I really dislike feeling out of control of my time, so I get it back under control as soon as possible.

Q. What advice can you offer to others of your type regarding time management?

I have a hard time imagining that any INTJs need much help with time management. If I had to give advice it would be to get away alone once every month or two and look at calendar issues and plan things to do.

Q. What help would you like to get regarding time management from others of your type?

None. But I would be very happy to get a copy of your research.

Eugene

INTJs might use their intuition to see what needs to be done quickly and thus save time that way. Also, the 'TJ' is a natural inclination for scheduling.

Gayle

I don't know that I can help you. I really don't have time management problems. In fact, I find that the more I have on my plate, the better I manage my time. When I was in grad school, I did a much better job managing my time when I was working two jobs and carrying a full time load than I did when I was only working one job. I'm a planner so I usually know how I'm going to spend my time and I budget my time in advance. I am the kind of person who completes projects ahead of deadline. I do get somewhat stressed when something throws my plans off and I have to work it into my schedule. I can't really think of any advice I would like from others regarding time management.

Stan

Here are my responses:

A successful time management experience:
• Went to a remote location. Took all I needed to exist until project was completed and took a single project to work on.

Difficulties:
• So much mail
• So many projects
• So many interests

• So multi-faceted
• So multi-talented

Advice for others:
• Call when you know you won't reach a talkative person and leave a specific voice mail or answering machine message. Saves a lot of time in some instances.

• Clearly establish #1 priority and stay with it till completion. Be focused.

Sally

Q. Tell me about an occasion when you felt really successful in managing your time.

I feel really successful when I make a 'to do list' and complete everything in the allotted time.

Q. Tell me about some of your difficulties in time management.

I often don't know how long it will take me to do something. I want the feeling of completion and am often afraid that I won't get it done in the time I have.

Q. What advice can you offer others of your type regarding time management?

I was in a homogeneous group of INTJ's just recently talking about work. Someone said they were focused on achievement, didn't care about what had been done in the past, once it was done, then they moved on to new achievements. I think that may be a common way of dealing with the world by INTJ's — but the down side is that you never pat yourself on the back for past achievements if that perception takes over. I would like to develop a way of expanding my perception so that I don't forget that I am an achiever.

Discussion

Although all of the INTJ contributors said they were successful with managing time, some of them shared two common difficulties: a frustration of interruptions, and a desire to procrastinate when the project is not inner-driven or interesting.

This is not surprising. According to type theory, the force that animates INTJs is the vision of inner-driven possibilities. Supported by their logic, and driven by an intense desire for achievement, they want to follow through on the development of their ideas, theories and principles. For INTJs, good time management is an integral part of their life's purpose.

Since the challenge of new accomplishments is what gives purpose to their lives, it is logical that they would be successful time managers. They can be very frustrated with interruptions because they want to concentrate intensely in order to satisfy their own high levels of achievement. They tend to procrastinate on uninteresting projects because they would rather concentrate on developing their own ideas and theories.

When asked to provide suggestions for others like themselves, most said they could not imagine an INTJ having difficulty with time management. Suggestions included ideas which suit the logical and planful INTJ work-style: "Use your natural inclination for scheduling." "Budget your time in advance." "Try to get away alone once every month or two and look at calendar issues and plan..." "Be focused!" "Clearly establish your #1 priority and stay with it till completion." "Use your intuition to see what needs to be done quickly and save time that way." "For routine tasks, use checklists to ensure that they get accomplished."

To deal with the frustration of interrupts, there were some practical ideas. "Call when you know you won't reach a talkative person and leave a specific message." "Be aware that something new might happen and throw your plans off; be prepared for this possibility."

One INTJ said that "we INTJs need to recognize our own achievement." Fulfilling intentions is important for INTJs because the driving force of their lives has to do with achievement.

As mentioned earlier, type should not be an excuse for behaviour. Rather, an understanding of a person's natural preferences can be helpful in the development of an effective style which embraces whatever provides the driving force and gives life its meaning. The contributors offered some useful suggestions to help INTJs to be even more effective time managers while still being themselves.

Helping INTJs Find their Own Way

Characteristics and behaviours which could be expected of an INTJ

- individualistic

- like to pioneer new pathways

- not much interested in following old routines

- have a strong drive

- like to develop long-range goals

- enjoy structuring step-by-step implementation

- appreciate efficient and effective use of resources

- work well independently

- approach objectives with single-minded intensity

- appreciate precision in communication

- expect efficiency when working with others

- have high standards for achievement

- may push themselves and others

- may lose patience with those who are less competent or efficient

- like to develop strategies and models

Driving forces
Intense desire for achievement resulting from inner-driven possibilities supported by logic.

Problems *most* likely to occur
Frustration with interruptions, desire to procrastinate when the project is not interesting.

Solutions *least* likely to be followed
Lower standards.

Suggestions

Here are a few suggestions that other INTJs found helpful.

1. Understand your need for concentrated alone-time.

- Try to get away alone once every month or two and look at calendar issues and plan things to do.

- Clearly establish your #1 priority and stay with it until completion.

2. Get routine tasks out of the way.

- Use your natural inclination for scheduling.

- Use checklists to ensure that routine tasks get completed.

- Use your intuition to see what needs to be done quickly and save time that way.

3. Be prepared for interruptions; try to avoid them if possible.

- Be aware that something new might happen and throw your plans off; be prepared for this possibility.

- Call when you know you won't reach a talkative person and leave a specific voice mail.

4. Consider alternatives.

- Think about how you can know when you have reached a level of excellence which satisfies you.

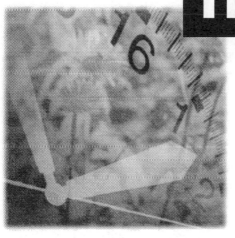

Chapter *12*

INTP

An Introduction to INTP

If you are an INTP, you probably have high (often escalating) standards for achievement. You value precision, efficiency and effectiveness and you trust logical reasoning. You like to solve complicated problems, do analysis and make strategic plans.

You value independence and self-determination. You work best when you have opportunities to set your own goals. You like flexible, unstructured time blocks and you need opportunities for privacy and quiet.

If a project is intriguing to you, you may become so mesmerized by it that you may work through the night. But if you do not find it interesting, you may find it difficult to stay motivated.

Time constraints can cause problems. You have so many ideas and you are so good at conceptualizing that sometimes you may be so preoccupied with this part of the project that you neglect to translate the concepts into actions. The project may be completed... but only in your own mind! This problem with follow-through may cause frustration for you and others.

With your many ideas and ability to make plans logically and consistently from beginning to end, you have the potential to make tremendous contributions... if only you can figure out how to actually implement your ideas within a real-life time frame.

I asked six INTPs how they cope with time management issues. These INTPs are not necessarily typical of their types, but their stories can provide helpful insights and ideas for you and for others. Several of them identify how they capitalize on the strengths which result from their type preferences, and several tell how they compensate for their natural weaknesses. Some tell of great frustrations and problems yet unsolved. Together they provide some useful suggestions for other INTPs.

Stories, Ideas, & Suggestions

Sandy

Q. Tell me about an occasion when you felt really successful in managing your time.

I do not often feel like I successfully manage my time and have few examples of when I've done it successfully, other than to have a day when I feel like I have accomplished a great deal because I was in the 'zone.' In other words, thoughts and ideas flowed freely, there were few interruptions, and I finished projects that I had spent a great deal of time thinking about.

Q. Tell me about some of your difficulties in time management.

These are a few difficulties that I see. I very much like to go with the flow, doing tasks as they appeal to me. I only make lists when I have to remember something, but as helpful as it is to have a list or a reminder, I even balk at the effort it takes to pick up the paper and pencil to write something down most of the time. (Sadly, good ideas can fade away!) I enjoy organizing ideas—I do not like organizing people or things and !hate! details.

I also enjoy the pressure of a deadline and often times find myself unable to sit down and commit to do the work until the deadline is approaching— this is when you will get my 'best work.' When I don't have deadlines and in order to jump-start myself at times, I create a fake 'crisis,' in other words I tell myself that this is an emergency, and I must do the work right now.

I do postpone decisions until I have enough information and enjoy work that allows me to be the 'consultant' without having to be the final decision maker. Thankfully, I am working in a position that allows me to do this.

Q. What advice can you offer to others of your type regarding time management?

Advice I would give to other INTPs is to organize your work and life in broad categories, leaving the details for someone else. Delegate!

Darlene

Q. *Tell me about an occasion when you felt really successful in managing your time.*

When I first hired a Personal Coach and we engaged in a 'clarification of important life values' exercise that gave me an easy-to-use tool to prioritize my activities/time. i.e., health stuff first, relationship with daughter next, authenticity (no compromises of values); independence (take care of clients); full self expression (don't join groups where I can't); peace and quiet (be aggressive about time for); inner integration (most of my activities contribute to personal development), etc.

Difficulties...

I'm creative and love to chase new concepts/activities/adventures. Doing this, I lose myself and sense of time.

Advice to other INTPs...

a) Hire a personal coach.

b) Be patient with yourself, you naturally dwell in the future.

Help from others...

Success stories from other INTPs!

Postscript:

My MBTI score is more like INXP. In my corporate life I practised as a 'T'. Since becoming independent, I hang out in 'F' more often.

Also, due to an increasing number of electronic toys, my 'N': 'when all else fails read the directions' attitude shifts to an 'S' posture. But of course, can't stay there for long!

P.S. *"In order to see, we have to stop being in the middle of the picture"*
—Sri Aurobindo

Ann Marie

Successes...

Once, I had a huge event where I was using Myers-Briggs with 130 individuals who worked with a large company. They all had to be typed in advance. In addition, I created an experiential learning session with 'brain teasers' to think out of the box. I also tied type to a fully interactive presentation highlighting effective teamwork, leadership and communication skills as they related to individual type. Needless to say, there were many details. I relied on a colleague that is an ESTJ to help organize and get things 'cooking'. I allowed the help which is not always easy to do as an INTP. I turned the help into a 'plus' by using it as a challenge to focus and 'get the job done'. I sometimes have the tendency, depending on how passionate I am about something I am doing to 'spin' the project in so many directions to make sure I provide the most value to the client, that I sometimes make it more difficult than it is, often times wanting to leave things 'open ended' until the last minute 'just in case'! With the help of the ESTJ, I followed her lead and it helped me see the value of getting things done 'now' rather than 'later' and the materials for the conference went out a week ahead of schedule which almost scared me... it has set me up for a 'best practices' on my other ongoing projects. The key... view the teamwork and different styles as a gift instead of a hindrance.

Difficulties...

• Wanting 'it' to be so perfect I either delay the start or make myself crazy with research before I actually get to the process of doing it.

• Wanting to change things so that they are innovative and are constantly adding value. I tend toward customizing and sometimes the added value is not sufficient for the 'pain and suffering' it causes (usually me!)

• Thinking ten hours work of work can fit in two. Realizing they can't. Driving myself crazy unnecessarily. Finally determining that it only took one and a half hours once I got started and that it was a breeze, but I don't come to that conclusion until I am 'fried!'

• Having a brilliant mind that sometimes betrays me in that it conceptualizes in my mind so clearly but then when I get to implementation, there is a disconnect, because I feel since I conceptualized it... I am done!

- In the scheme of things... thinking that the 'pie of life' carved into five slices is solely dedicated to work. Therefore I am out of balance when 80% of my time is work time and there is little to no down time or play time. So much so, that if there is down or play time, I turn it into a chore!

- Making the project 'in my mind' appear more immense than it is... to the point of being overwhelmed before I start... therefore I delay the start.

- Over-promising, with the best of intentions due to the disconnect between conceptualizing and implementing.

- Not making enough time to carry out the things I must do. I think it so therefore it is done. Then to my surprise, 'done' takes longer than conceptualizing!

- Want to rescue, help, mentor, train, be customer-focused... and forgetting that I am my own customer as well.

Advice to others...

- First... get a life... seriously! I started to put one personal activity a week in my calendar to start balancing out. What I put in, had to be done! No questions!

- If something is due tomorrow, make believe it is due today and whether you have to kick and scream through it emotionally, start. I don't care if you start in the middle... start. Start rambling on the computer or paper and then go back to it and you will find, to your surprise, a framework you can live with.

- Make sure you make time to create and then time to see your 'creation' through!

- Be humble enough to ask for help!

- Don't give exact deadlines, if possible. Say it can be done the week of... or next week... or no later than... This will give you the motivation and flexibility that you need to stay motivated to see something through.

- Be realistic about your scheduling. Where did you book time for you?

- Set aside one day a week as 'braintrust' day for you to catch up, organize, create, process information, make calls, send e-mails... in other words get the creative juices flowing again.

- Understand the gifts of other types and capitalize on them.

- Read as much as you can about your type and the things you seek and avoid so that you can help yourself... knowledge is power!

- Make time to play so you can go the distance.

- Eat well. This was very important to me. I did not realize how important this is.

- Find your ideal time of the day to work and honour it. Whether that is early, early am like me or late at night.

- Don't tire yourself out. Again, honour your natural pace.

- Learn to say no... gently. You can always negotiate a deadline and it will work out beautifully when you put yourself first and honour what you offer as career gifts. Often times, we say 'yes' and then figure out how to do it.

- Figure out how it can be done before you say yes! Ask for input!

- Have a realistic sense of time and space. When you find yourself in a pinch (and it still happens to me)... ask yourself, "How can I make this less complicated?" Also remind yourself constantly "this is good enough!" Our 80% is someone else's 200%. This is sometimes more a curse than a gift. INTPs know what I mean by this. Enough is enough already!

- Finally, honour the fact that sometimes we wait until the 'almost' last minute because it forces our minds to focus and to not 'spin' as much. Realize that you can get the job done, where others would be panicking, stay cool and enjoy the process rather than freak out over it.

Help needed from others...

- How they find balance.

- How they meet tight deadlines.

- How they can help themselves get to places on time without making that stressful as well.

- Planning ahead without stressing out (sometimes this feels worse than waiting).

- Tips to enjoy the work process a little more.

- Ways they have honoured their work pace and style and found ways to benefit from it rather than be restricted by it.

Avis

I've used every time management tool out there. Covey, Franklin, Daytime, Outlook, MS Schedule. I enjoy the quest of researching what the various tools provide for me. I am totally undisciplined when it comes to utilizing the tools. Not to mention when your favourite isn't supported any longer. I use Lotus Notes at work and I'm experimenting with that tool and don't think it will help me. I have to work very hard to stay on top of planning. Goal setting, planners, 'to do lists' are something I believe to be important, but I have difficulty finding the time to implement them on a regular basis. I have started lightening up on myself. I carry my Franklin and I have weekly pages in it but I generally don't start my day and plan it. I generally refer to it quickly to check on appointments I'm pretty sure I know already exist.

Terry

I am very poor at time management. I find that I am easily diverted to other activities while I should be managing my time better. I really think we have an obsession with so-called time management to a point that has become pathological. In this ever busier world we live in we have created many devices that are supposed to save us time, with the inherent assumption that we will then have more time to do 'useful and productive things.'

For instance FAX machines are supposed to allow us to communicate more directly and save time doing so. In practice, most people leave things to the last minute and then send us urgent faxes that disrupt what we were doing. With this urgent fax is the need for an urgent reply, which of course involves further work that takes us away from what we were supposed to be doing.

The same situation exists for e-mail and electronic transfer of documents. With these electronic marvels we can now allow others to make instant demands on our time so that they, in practice, manage our time for us. I really think that the concept that we can effectively manage our time is a myth. One level of management makes demands on the next level down and so it goes. All our electronic 'productivity' tools only accelerate the rate of chaos around us.

When was the last time that any of had the luxury of going off alone to a quiet space and really getting something done that we intended to do? Fax machines, voice mail, electronic mail, electronic document routing and transfers and telephones have their place but they and others using them are the real managers of our time in the workplace of the 90's. I relish the days that I can spend at my home office really working and managing my time. The productivity and output is better than anything that I can achieve In my electronic workplace.

I don't know what this has to do with MBTI type, but I do know that I would like to have less of my time managed than more. Perhaps this Is my dominant introverted mode crying out for solitude and real time to stop and think and turn some of our overflow of information into wisdom.

April

I manage my time somewhat as a 'J' preference might. I need to keep a calendar and use an organizer for this. I keep track of what has to be done when. I also keep a Monday - Friday file and keep the work for the day in the designated day. This way, I know what has to get done. I also try to get the mundane work done quickly to allow me more time to do the fun work.

I back into my deadlines so I know what has to get started when. I do a lot of writing and a lot of it is done in my head before I ever sit down to the computer. I don't wait to the last minute but work ahead - to allow me time if anything really interesting comes up and I can go off. It seems to work well for me.

I appreciate deadlines and have made it practice to meet them. I do a lot of grant work which requires that you be on time. No extensions are allowed. I try to be cognizant of other people's needs as well and the interim times help me stay on track.

I've had a boss that really believed I was a 'J' to her 'P'. While I can function in business that way, I had to examine my motives for doing so rather than it being just a behaviour. It is a matter of being competent - if I meet them we stand a chance of getting money and that provides a sense of competence. I also, as I said above, do it so that I have flexibility in case something better comes up that I don't have to pass it up.

Hope this helps.

Discussion

INTP

Most of the INTP contributors were really struggling with time management, and this was causing many of them great frustration and stress. Success stories resulted from behaving in ways that are not natural for this type, enlisting the help of others with other strengths, or hiring a personal coach.

This was not surprising. According to type theory, the force that animates INTPs is the inner need to analyze the world, not to run it. INTPs feel compelled to generate original ideas and build complex conceptual models, but they do not feel driven to get the ideas implemented.

When asked to provide suggestions for others like themselves, they offered advice which would enable INTPs to keep generating those wonderful ideas while still somehow meeting the demands of the workplace. (In one person's case, this seemed so impossible that he just poured out his frustrations.)

Some suggestions had to do with dealing with the discord between what INTPs feel driven to do by their inner needs, and what they have to do because of their jobs, and what is best for their health. "Be patient with yourself. You naturally dwell in the future so you have to work harder than other people to do everyday tasks." "Set aside one day a week to catch up, organize, create, process information, make calls, and generally revitalize." "Take care of yourself so you can keep up your energy and health." "Remember that INTPs tend to work exhaustively. Midway through a project, stop and ask yourself if you are overdoing or over-complicating the work. Perhaps the project can be simplified and the deadline met." "Try to figure out how you can create the quiet space that you need to work in an uninterrupted way..." "Set aside some peaceful time for yourself where you can synthesize all of those wonderful ideas and plans which you have." "Include personal activities and fun on your calendar so that you don't go overboard with one project."

In order to meet the demands of the workplace, a few practical suggestions were offered: "Pretend the deadline is ahead of when it actually is." "Force yourself to start actually implementing the work." "Ask for help when you need it. Capitalize on people of other types." "Organize your life in broad categories, leaving the details for someone else." "Don't lock yourself into unrealistic deadlines. Try to build enough flexibility into your plans because things usually take longer than you thought." "Find your ideal time of day and honour it." "Think before you agree to do something. You may have to say 'no'... gently, after you realize how much time it will actually take."

As mentioned earlier, type should not be an excuse for behaviour. Rather, an understanding of a person's natural preferences can be helpful in the development of an effective style which embraces whatever provides the driving force and gives life its joy. The contributors, by recognizing what is important in their own lives, were able to offer some useful suggestions to help INTPs.

Helping INTPs Find their Own Way

Characteristics and behaviours which could be expected of an INTP

- have high (often escalating) standards for achievement

- value precision

- value efficiency

- trust logical reasoning

- like to solve complicated problems

- enjoy analysis

- like making strategic plans

- value independence

- like to set own goals

- appreciate flexible, unstructured time blocks

- need opportunities for privacy and quiet

- may become mesmerized by a project which is interesting

- may have difficulty with motivation if something is not interesting

- good at conceptualizing

- sometimes have problems with follow-through

Driving forces
To generate complex ideas and build conceptual models.

Problems *most* likely to occur
Losing interest, getting distracted, not following through to completion.

Solutions *least* likely to be followed
Carefully follow a routine.

Suggestions

Here are some suggestions which will enable you to keep generating those wonderful ideas while still somehow meeting the demands of the workplace.

1. Understand your own style of working.

- Be patient with yourself. You naturally dwell in the future, so you have to work harder than other people to do everyday tasks.

- Organize your work and life in broad categories, leaving the details for someone else (if you can).

- Don't lock yourself into unrealistic deadlines. Try to build enough flexibility into your plans because things usually take longer than you thought.

- Try to figure out how you can create the quiet space that you need to work in an uninterrupted way.

- Set aside some peaceful time for yourself where you can synthesize all of those wonderful ideas and plans which you have.

2. Try to develop some structure.

- Set aside one day a week to catch up, organize, create, process information, make calls, and generally revitalize

- Find your ideal time of the day to work and honour it.

- Force yourself to start actually implementing the plan.

- Pretend the deadline is ahead of when it actually is.

- Consider hiring a personal coach to help you with time planning. Make sure your own personal needs are considered in the plans.

- Think before you agree to do something. You may have to say 'no...' gently, after you realize how much time it will actually take.

3. Get help from others.

- Capitalize on people of other types.

4. Know your tendency to work exhaustively.

- Include personal activities and fun on your calendar so that you don't go overboard with one project.

- Midway through a project, stop and ask yourself if you are overdoing or over-complicating the work. Perhaps the project can be simplified and the deadline met.

- Take care of yourself so you can keep up your energy and health.

Chapter *13*

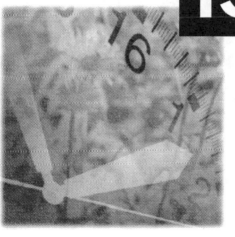

ISFJ

An Introduction to ISFJ

If you are an ISFJ, you are likely to be extremely systematic and thorough in your approach to work. You are dependable and stable, and appear to be calm even in emergency situations, providing warmth and reassurance to those who need it. Privately, you can be very individualistic and original.

You appreciate a work environment which is stable and orderly, and at the same time characterized by supportiveness, harmony, and camaraderie. You pay careful attention to what other people want and need, sometimes ignoring your own needs in the process.

You have a deep sense of responsibility, a commitment to deadlines, and a respect for details. Sometimes this can cause you to take on too much work and get overloaded and exhausted. Your efforts to always do your best may also result in stress. You have a strong sense of duty and expect the same of others.

You work best when things are predictable and when time-tested values are used. You appreciate clear, step-by-step instructions, and established routines. You like a private, orderly, uncluttered workspace where there is a minimum of interruptions.

Your desire to serve may make it difficult for you to say 'no.' As a result other people may take advantage of your kindness and good will, and depend on you rather than doing things for themselves.

I asked five ISFJs how they try to cope with time management. These ISFJs are not necessarily typical of their types, but their stories can provide helpful information for you and others. Several identify how they make the most of the strengths which result from their type preferences, and several tell how they compensate for their natural weaknesses. Some tell of difficulties yet unsolved. Together they provide some unique ideas and useful suggestions for ISFJs.

Stories, Ideas, & Suggestions

Julie

Hi! Thanks for the opportunity to chat with you.

Q. *Tell me about an occasion when you felt really successful in managing your time.*

I feel really successful managing my time at home. A recent occasion was planning my son's Halloween party with nine children. Given the activity was task-oriented, I managed the activities and the schedule of the party quite well.

Q. *Tell me about some of your difficulties in time management.*

If I have difficulty, it's when I have too much to juggle. This occurs most often in trying to juggle my home responsibilities and my workload. It gets so overwhelming that I go blank in what and how things should be prioritized. If activities tend to be too conceptual in their thinking for me I will tend to procrastinate on them until I can't put it off any longer or I have finally thought it through in my head how I'm going to approach it.

Advice to others:

Try not to be a perfectionist when it comes to time management. Know when to let go of things. Know that not everything will get done in your time-frame. Flexibility and patience help a lot.

Betsy

Hi! Sorry I waited so long to respond, but I have been home recovering from surgery and was moving slowly there for awhile. As far as my time management skills, I would say that my biggest problem is Procrastination. I am a paralegal at a law firm and work in the area of trademark prosecution (filing applications, writing letters to foreign trademark agents, preparing time sensitive documents) and about 90% of my day is based on managing my time and meeting deadlines. Each legal assistant has at least 100 clients and receives a monthly docket with all his/her deadlines spelled out for the next three month period. I do well with this system, but do find that I procrastinate doing the tougher tasks and quickly attend to the simpler tasks thinking that if I get the majority of the workload out of the way I will have more time to think about the more challenging tasks. This system causes those tougher tasks to pile up and cause STRESS. I would say that the most successful time management situation at this job is any time I am going to be out for any length of time, whether it is a vacation, or in my recent case, 2-3 months, for surgery. I have to start planning on being out sometimes weeks ahead so that things don't fall through the cracks while I'm gone, or I don't leave too many things for others to handle in my absence. This usually requires a lot of overtime prior to being out of the office, since we all have a very heavy load. I am very conscientious and hate leaving my work for someone else to do. In fact, I have felt guilty since my surgery that others are having to help me.

I can't really give advice for others. I have been at this current job for so long that I do have a handle on it, but it is always stressful due to the workload.

Susan

I apologize for the delay. My father was very ill and passed away recently. Hence, this request was set aside. Here are my responses to the questions:

Q. Tell me about a time when you were really successful at time management.

I am particularly successful when I am handling multiple projects simultaneously. The specific situation relates to spring 1998. As a full-time graduate student, I was taking 11 hours of course-work, working 20 hours/ week and orchestrating my marriage and domestic responsibilities. In school most of my course-work involved a lot of detail, there were stated deadlines, known expected outcomes and the results were tangible. With respect to the projects, there was discretion in topics and I was able to decide topics quickly, identify key decisions to be made and establish an initial framework for the project. With a limited time-frame to accomplish the projects, it required steady work and the design of the projects required good research.

Q. Tell me about your difficulties in time management.

Time management difficulties include the fact I can decide too quickly and may not allocate time to the right issue or aspect; I tend to do what's comfortable first regardless whether it's the most effective and efficient; I find it difficult to draw a line and not continue to dig for details and consequently get too much into the muck when I need to be at a higher (bigger picture) level. Lastly, when I'm writing, I write and rewrite and rewrite again so I say things exactly correctly. I also find it difficult to remain flexible in taking in more information or changing my path.

Advice to others:

a) Don't let timetables and initial decisions limit your thinking.

b) Push yourself to continually take in more information.

c) Relax and allow yourself to dream and enjoy spurts of spontaneity.

Jerry

I am really struggling trying to describe a time when I felt successful managing time. After all these years you would think it come easily to me. But I describe myself as time bound. I make lists and more lists and then I feel good when I scratch something off as DONE! This is a curse. I am always checking my watch or a clock, everything is related to making effective use of a valuable resource... which of course is time.

I always have multiple things going on. It's difficult to set priorities because to me everything on my list is important. This attitude has created tension and stress in my life and career, however as I have matured I am under control, more relaxed and have even been described recently as laid back.

What am I doing? Well, at work I don't try to read everything in detail that comes across my desk, I have learned to 'chuck' a lot of 'junk' into the trash, or if need be, come back and peruse it later.

I have learned to delegate. I have assumed more of a mantle of Leadership and have learned to empower my colleagues instead of trying to control things by doing it all myself. This requires trusting yourself, then you can trust others and it also requires looking honestly at yourself and admitting that you are a perfectionist and your prime motivation has been fear of failure. But more importantly, you have to be able to laugh at yourself, be humble and quit taking yourself so seriously.

If I could give any advice I would say 'give up control.' Then we all grow in ways you can't imagine and most importantly... I am repeating myself... laugh.

Ruth

Q. Tell me about an occasion when you felt really successful in managing your time.

When I completed a project without allowing interruptions (phone messages, e-mails, drop-ins) to prevent timely completion.

Q. Tell me about an occasion when you felt really successful in managing your time.

I have the tendency to take care of the quick jobs despite their priority and not get to those things that require more concentration. I then do that on the weekends and spend more time on the weekends than I sometimes would like doing work.

Q. What advice can you offer to others of your type regarding time management?

Plan but be flexible, set aside time for the priority projects to ensure completion.

I hope this helps!

Discussion

The ISFJ contributors tended to be friendly, chatty, and reliable in generally providing prompt replies to the research questions.

Although most of the ISFJ contributors could tell at least one successful time management story, they seemed to share a common difficulty: taking on too much work.

With a clear inner sense of reality, supported by their feeling to serve others, and driven by a strong desire to see tangible results, ISFJs are willing to get things organized and done. For ISFJs, good time management is an integral part of their life's purpose.

Since completing things well is so important to their lives, it is logical that they would try so hard to be successful time managers. They can be very frustrated when something interferes with their careful plans.

The contributors to this study understood this. When asked to provide suggestions for others like themselves, most suggested ways to let go of some control. "Try not to be a perfectionist when it comes to time management. Know when to let go of things." "Try to reduce your workload by off-loading some of it and try not to feel guilty about it!" "Try to learn to delegate; give yourself an opportunity to empower others, instead of trying to control things by yourself." "Try to give up some control so you can grow in other ways, laugh and enjoy life." "Know that not everything will get done in your time-frame. Flexibility and patience help a lot." "Don't let timetables and initial decisions limit your thinking."

There were also suggestions to reduce the workload by prioritizing tasks. "Try to avoid wasting time on tasks that are not useful in the long run; get on with the important things." "Plan but be flexible, set aside time for the priority projects to ensure completion."

To further reduce the workload (and the stress), there were suggestions to take life a little less seriously: "Look honestly at yourself. If you are a perfectionist, perhaps your prime motivation has been fear of failure. Remember, you can't trust others until you first learn to trust yourself." "Relax and allow yourself to dream and enjoy spurts of spontaneity."

As mentioned earlier, type should not be an excuse for behaviour. Rather, an understanding of a person's natural preferences can be helpful in the development of an effective style which embraces whatever provides the driving force and gives life its meaning. The contributers offered some useful suggestions to help ISFJs continue to meet their goals without taking on too much work.

Helping ISFJs Find their Own Way

Characteristics and behaviours which could be expected of an ISFJ

- systematic
- thorough
- dependable
- stable
- appear to be calm even in emergency situations
- like an orderly work environment
- appreciate supportiveness, harmony, and camaraderie when working with others
- attentive to what other people want and need
- sometimes ignor own needs

- have a deep sense of responsibility
- feel committed to deadlines
- respect details
- may take on too much work
- appreciate clear, step-by-step instructions
- appreciate established routines
- like a private, orderly, uncluttered workspace
- do not like too many interruptions
- may find it hard to say 'no'

Driving forces
To get things organized and done, especially in the service of others.

Problems *most* likely to occur
Taking on too much work.

Solutions *least* likely to be followed
Don't work so hard.

Suggestions

Here are some suggestions which will enable you to keep managing your time well while reducing your workload a little.

1. Think about your priorities.

- Plan but be flexible, set aside time for the priority projects to ensure completion.
- Try to avoid wasting time on tasks that are not useful in the long run; get on with the important things.

2. Look at schedules and timetables a little less rigidly.

- Try not to be quite so much of a perfectionist when it comes to time management. Know that not everything will get done in your time-frame. Flexibility and patience help a lot.
- Don't let timetables and initial decisions limit your thinking.

3. Try to let go of some control.

- Try to reduce your workload by off-loading some of it and try not to feel guilty about it!
- Give yourself an opportunity to empower others by delegating, instead of trying to control things by yourself.
- Try to give up some control so you can grow in other ways, laugh and enjoy life.
- Relax once in a while and allow yourself to dream and enjoy spurts of spontaneity.

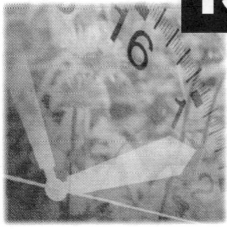

Chapter **14**

ISFP

An Introduction to ISFP

If you are an ISFP, you want more out of work and life than just a paycheque or material reward. You work best if it is for a purpose or people you truly care about or if it is in response to an urgent need.

To work joyfully and well, you need to have freedom to choose how you want to do things. You are a free spirit, and you feel unhappy if others try to cramp your style. You can work well individually or with a few people whom you like. You enjoy working spontaneously.

When you are committed to the task, you work hard to do the best you can. You appreciate opportunities to enhance your skills. You want to see tangible and aesthetically pleasing results. You believe it is important to appreciate and enjoy the moment and may create ways to make a task more enjoyable if you can.

You may have your own creative style of organizing things. In planning for the future, you generally prefer not to look too far ahead, and appreciate living one day at a time. You are able to be quite effective in getting people to work with you toward an important cause.

I asked six ISFPs how they try to cope with time management. These ISFPs are not necessarily typical of their types, but their stories can provide helpful information for you and others. Several identify how they make the most of the strengths which result from their type preferences, and several tell how they compensate for their natural weaknesses. Some tell of difficulties yet unsolved. Together they provide some unique ideas and useful suggestions for ISFPs.

Stories, Ideas, & Suggestions

Alan

Hi Sharon. Brief answers okay?

Q. *Tell me about an occasion when you felt really successful in managing your time.*

(Should I count the time I ignored responding to a survey about time management?)

As manager of a summer camp facility for disabled persons funded by private donations, we were about to be visited by several media and donor representatives. Along with our 28 hour a day work to do, we had to prepare certain 'niceties' for the dignitaries. Impossible by oneself, so I gathered our small overworked staff together, gave them a pep-talk, and then proceeded to assign them certain tasks to be done by the next day. The call to arms was answered very well by the troops, so while they were sleeping I prepared a celebration for them on their day off to thank them for their extra hard work and job well-done. Delegation and reward. Take that to the bank.

Q. *Tell me about some of your difficulties in time management.*

I manage time best when I 'think' and there are others to 'do'. If I stop to 'do,' I lose concentration on the big picture and get lost in little side-tracking details. If I must do it myself, I must give myself a schedule and stick to it. Reward if on time, personal penalty ('only one gin and tonic for you today') if late. Even simple things need a schedule. For example, if I wake up and don't hit the shower immediately, I will most certainly be late for work. Eating before shower never works, because I will take too long and not get in the shower soon enough. If I stay in the predetermined 'shower first, fun later' (Hmmm, all sorts of implications...) schedule, I am guaranteed to be on time. Making a schedule (routine) and sticking to it works for me.

Q. *What advice can you offer to others of your type regarding time management?*

As above, 'delegation and reward'. If by myself, 'routine and reward'. Do the most important things first, then proceed in order. Make lists so that you don't stray from the order, and leave space in-between items to fill in 'to-do's' that inevitably arise.

Then... have a good time!

Karen

Hi Sharon, I hope this helps you:

Successes at managing time:

A while ago, I had four or five projects on the go. Two of them had tight time lines. I managed to get both of the demanding projects done, and just under the required time limits. I made lists of what had to be done each day, big tasks and even the very small ones, so that I wouldn't forget anything. I took enjoyment in crossing each task off.

Difficulties at managing time:

I can be forgetful at times. So making lists really helps me. My work environment is the only place I make them, but is very helpful.

I often put off things I don't like doing, or don't want to do, so I try to do those things first. This makes sure I do them and not forget about them. I usually have to stop myself when I am putting unwanted tasks aside and just do them.

I also find that I am scattered in my tasks. I will start one thing, and remember something else, and attend to the new task, before I forget about it. So sometimes, I have a lot of things going on at the same time, but nothing is really getting finished. I have to consciously keep focused at the tasks at hand, and try to forget the other matters that need to be taken care of, unless of course it is urgent.

Overall, I think knowing where my problems are in time management, really help me. But I have to find those problems and deal with them. Kind Regards.

Patricia

Successes at managing time:

To date, I have yet to feel successful with my time management.

Difficulties at managing time:

a. Organization.

b. Prioritization.

c. Moving on to another project prior to finishing a previous set of projects.

d. Motivation.

Advice to other ENFJs:

Find a tool to assist in overcoming the difficulties and continue to assess your degrees of success. I hope this is helpful.

Bob

Q. Tell me about an occasion when you felt really successful in managing your time.

In general, I feel most successful in managing my time when the conditions include a sense of urgency, deadlines to be met, importance, and challenge. One of several specific examples that can relate came on the heals of a budget driven decision that eliminated my position and those of my counselling colleagues last year. There was a relatively short window of opportunity in which to solicit support, prepare counter arguments, and at the very least let it be known how much we disagreed with the decision. Other routine job responsibilities were not completely ignored but priorities were easily established and fighting for our jobs was clearly the winner. The whole effort was very energizing and satisfying because I believed strongly that our position was correct and widely supported. When the final decision was a done deal, even though the outcome was not completely to my satisfaction, I was pleased with the effort and that much had been accomplished in the time available. A certain fatigue then set in that had accumulated over the course of the project but that had not hindered getting things done at the time.

Q. Tell me about some of your difficulties in time management.

Time management difficulties often include getting started on a task, in particular those that lack the above mentioned sense of importance or urgency. I am capable of putting off or delaying getting fully started, knowing that I will nevertheless complete on time (I rarely will miss a deadline). If others are participants, I can be impatient with their pace or progress although I will rarely verbalize these concerns, and may just take the initiative and get on with it myself. I often find it more difficult to manage time when I am the sole beneficiary of the task, whereas I can readily get things done for others who I care about.

Advice to other ISFPs:

- Projecting how much time a task requires may be challenging. I try to take advantage of guidelines or recommendations if available, and rely on past experience doing similar activities.

- Finding personal meaning - why should the task in question be important to me, or to others who may be depending on my contribution - as a motivating force.

I hope this is helpful - good luck with the research and I will look forward to your findings as I can see how they could be of benefit to the students I work with here at the college.

D.C.

Q. Tell me about an occasion when you felt really successful in managing your time.

Perhaps one example when I believe that I managed my time effectively and efficiently was about four years ago when our executive secretary had to leave work because of stress. For six months I managed her full time job, my full time job (I'm an administrative assistant), and a part time evening and weekend job that I had at the time. During that period

I managed to fulfill all of the responsibilities associated with three positions, meet all deadlines, and avoid murdering anyone.

For five and a half years I worked at two jobs (one full and one part time), took dance lessons, did aerobics, cycled and hiked and still managed to run a house so I must manage my time somewhat, although it doesn't feel like I'm making a concerted effort to do so.

I'm never late for appointments, meetings or social engagements. I always meet deadlines and time-lines; I work best when I'm very busy and under pressure—otherwise, I procrastinate.

Q. Tell me about some of your difficulties in time management.

As I said above, if it isn't essential, I tend to put it off. I usually don't have any structure—I just kind of know what to do and eventually do it. For example, I often intend to do housework on a Saturday morning but instead sit down with a book and coffee or talk on the phone to a friend.

I prioritize, but in an informal sort of way. That is, when I have a number of jobs to do, I have the habit of allocating portions of time in my head in which to complete each task—and thereby knowing 'exactly how long it will take to get everything done.' However, either the amounts of time I allocate are unrealistic or I get sidetracked along the way so that I never get the whole thing done in the amount of time which thought I could. I often leave things to the last minute and then work like a demon to get them done (if I have to).

Unless things are absolutely critical, I don't tend to worry about them. If I'm tired and want to watch TV, I do. As you've probably guessed, I don't have high blood pressure! The problem is that sometimes I don't get some things which are semi-critical done—like I don't quite get to the grocery shopping part of my day because I've spent the entire morning reading. In such cases I just sort of wing it—I buy what we need immediately.

I don't, of course, plan menus ahead of time and shop in accordance with that. I'm not particularly good about planning my day ahead of time— either at home or at work. I kinda know what I'm supposed to do and I do it, but it's not a really organized strategy.

I am absolutely reliable with deadlines, but, at work, when I have a task which needs to be done 'soon' or 'sometime' and it doesn't appeal to me, I just put it off until it becomes critical—then I get it done. I don't think or plan or worry about work when I'm not there; I'm always surprised when I hear my co-workers say that they do.

Q. What advice can you offer to others of your type regarding time management?

What I feel that I should say is that I should try to:

a. Make actual lists of tasks (I've never made a list—even a grocery list—in my entire life).

b. Try to complete those tasks in an orderly fashion—and *then* read a book!

c. Plan ahead more.

d. Do more things ahead of time, rather than leaving them until they absolutely have to be done.

e. Appear to be more organized.

Many people don't really like my work or time management style because it doesn't seem that I have a system and don't appear to worry about it. It creates some problems for both my husband and my boss; however, my boss concedes that I'm very reliable (it just doesn't appear that I am).

I tend to work with a messy desk—I keep everything that I need on top of it until I don't need it any more, then I file it. However, I always know exactly what's on top of my desk and where to find it. It's not that I'm sloppy—I really don't like to put things away until they're complete. Sometimes I sort of wish I could appear to be more organized, but I never get around to it!

I once had a co-worker who was the exact opposite of me. Before she actually started doing any work, she took the time to organize everything into folders—with labels—and filed those away. She always completed one task entirely before beginning another. Her desk was always totally bare and her office very, very, very tidy and neat. I was amazed since I thought that taking the time to do all of that preparatory organization was a total waste of time—it seemed to me that she could have completed two or three tasks in the time it took her to organize them! She was the person who needed stress leave, so...

I don't make lists, write reminders to myself or put anniversary and birth dates in a little book—but I should! I should also make the best use of every day, but I don't. I waste a lot of time—but it doesn't particularly bother me.

Carol

Q. Tell me about an occasion when you felt really successful in managing your time.

I'm best at time management if there is a little outside pressure, for example a deadline, or someone coming over, therefore you have a short time span to get everything spiffy, or you are leaving and have a number of things to accomplish before going somewhere.

I am not currently working out of the home so my best example involves preparation for a two week volunteer job out of town. My husband was going to be away for part of the time as well, leaving a dog, and a 20 year old at home. Tasks that have comfortably been put off for ages now need to be done in say four days. Some action has occurred over a two week lead up to departure, like studying for the test that will be written while away, and some of the yard and housework tasks, since I like to leave things clean and tidy inside and out when I go.

I work best if I can do several tasks at once so the final days before departure are a flurry of little bits of everything. I clean cupboards for 20 minutes, throw in laundry, go outside and do yard work until I'm bored or tired and then do another cupboard inside. I study synchro for awhile, read and watch videos, and then head out for more work in the garden or yard.

Then I may come in and snack and read a novel for ten minutes. I squeeze in visits to friends and my regular activities as well as the frenzy of cleaning and even find a minute or two to rewrite the wills and have them signed. Grocery shopping to stock-up the larder for my daughter and the dog gets done too. Finally packing and going to the airport. That sounds a little nuts but it worked very well for me and everything gets done.

I have two fairly distinct styles. One is free, intense, and chaotic as outlined above and one is very focused and committed to completion. If

I feel I have to, for whatever reason, I can do one task until it's done. I don't like doing that though. I am much happier allowing myself to do a variety of things. It takes longer to do everything, of course, but it's much more fun.

Q. Tell me about some of your difficulties in time management.

Difficulties would be trying to justify my system to others, or having others helping. The help is alright if they do something with me in my mode or something by themselves that doesn't need my assistance or supervision but not if I have to defer to their way of doing things. Difficulties also arise if I haven't allowed enough time for all the last minute jobs. That's a little stressful but experience has allowed for fairly accurate projections of time.

In other situations, particularly in a study area, procrastination is also a difficulty. Without a deadline of some sort I often put things off forever or dabble but don't devote the time and concentration necessary for completion or mastery of a subject. I also have a streak of perfectionism, tied to wanting to do things quick and easy. As you can imagine they don't go together too well.

Q. What advice can you offer to others of your type regarding time management?

I'd advise others of my type to make a list, make several lists, then do what ever you feel like doing in whatever order. The list is merely a brainstorming exercise, not necessarily a preferred sequence.

I guess other suggestions would be to do it your way. Whether I'm a typical ISFP or not, I know despite its apparent drawbacks, doing several things at once works best for me. Setting up my own deadlines for a certain number of pages read and understood by a certain length of time (in several subjects at once, of course) help in overcoming the inclination to put off studying whatever I have chosen to learn or wish I knew.

Hope that is of some use to you.

Discussion

I was amused by the happy-go-lucky style of some of the ISFPs, yet underneath the laid-back exterior, there were good-hearted souls who didn't want to let you down.

Most of the ISFP contributors were able to tell at least one time management success story. But many seemed prone to distraction, forgetfulness, or procrastination when they did not feel any urgency or importance in the task.

This was not surprising. According to type theory, the force that animates ISFPs is the desire for harmony in the inner world of feeling. ISFPs deeply need to feel that their ideals are being lived in everything they do; otherwise the task is not worth doing - at least not right away.

The contributors to this study seemed to understand this. When asked to provide suggestions for others like themselves, they offered only ideas which would enable ISFPs to live in their own way, while not getting themselves in a bind or losing the confidence of others due to leaving things undone too long.

To keep from leaving things undone for too long, ISFPs need to feel motivated. If the motivation can not come from the nature of the task (if it doesn't really seem that urgent), then ISFPs would need to find some other way to motivate themselves. Suggestions included: "Make personal meaning a motivating force. Figure out why the task could be important to you, or to others who are depending on you." Three people suggested extrinsic rewards: "If working by yourself, routine and reward." "Do the work... then have a good time!" Another ISFP suggested trying to make the job more fun: "Do it your way! If doing several things at once works best for you, despite its apparent drawbacks, do it that way!"

There was also a little practical advice. "Do the most important things first, then proceed in order. Make lists so that you don't stray from that order. Leave space in between for new to-do's which arise..." The spaces would also allow for the ISFP's need to deal with urgent demands that often arise.

ISFPs were helped with self-discipline for cases where they know the task should be done but it is not that fun and does not seem urgent. One person provided this testimonial to show how procrastination can be overcome: "I stop myself when I begin to put aside tasks and just do them." Another person suggested that ISFPs should try to do what she believed she ought to do: "Plan ahead more, do more things ahead of time, rather than leaving them until they absolutely have to be done. Make lists of tasks. Complete these lists in an orderly fashion — and *then* read a book!" (Again, the reward of a pleasant activity.)

As mentioned earlier, type should not be an excuse for behaviour. Rather, an understanding of a person's natural preferences can be helpful in the development of an effective style which embraces whatever provides the driving force and gives life its joy and meaning. The contributors, by recognizing what is important in their own lives, were able to offer some useful suggestions to help ISFPs.

Helping ISFPs Find their Own Way

Characteristics and behaviours which could be expected of an ISFP

- want more out of life than just a paycheque
- work best if it is for a purpose or people they truly care about or if there is an urgent need
- need to have freedom to choose how to do things
- a free spirit
- unhappy if others try to cramp their style
- work well individually or with a few people whom they like
- enjoy working spontaneously
- hard-working when committed

- appreciate opportunities to enhance skills
- want tangible and aesthetically pleasing results
- believe it is important to appreciate and enjoy the moment
- may create ways to make a task more enjoyable
- may have their own creative style of organizing things
- generally prefer not to look too far ahead
- like to live one day at a time
- quite effective in recruiting people for a cause

Driving forces
To live according to values, to lend help when needed.

Problems *most* likely to occur
Distraction, forgetfulness, procrastination (if the task does not seem important).

Solutions *least* likely to be followed
Make a schedule and follow it carefully.

Suggestions

Here are some suggestions which may help you to live in your own way while avoiding getting in a bind or losing the confidence of others.

1. Try to find a way to motivate yourself, even if the task is not urgent.

- Make personal meaning a motivating force. Figure out why the task is important to you, or to others who may be depending on you.
- Complete the work, then reward yourself or have a good time.

2. Organize yourself a little to get tasks out of the way.

- Make lists to help you keep from putting off things you don't like doing.
- Do the most important things first, then proceed in order. Leave space in between for new 'to-do's' with arise.
- Make a list, or several lists, and then do whatever you feel like doing in whatever order.

- Do it your way! If doing several things at once works best for you, despite its apparent drawbacks, do it that way!
- Set up deadlines for yourself to overcome the inclination to put things off too long.
- Improve your ability to project how much time a task requires.
- Take advantage of guidelines or recommendations if available, or use your own past experience doing similar activities.

3. Try to keep yourself from getting distracted or procrastinating on jobs you don't want to do.

- Stop yourself when you find yourself putting aside tasks and just do them.

Chapter *15*

ISTJ

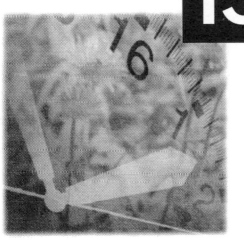

An Introduction to ISTJ

If you are an ISTJ, you are probably hard working and practical. You are systematic and thorough in your approach to tasks. You are outwardly matter-of-fact, but privately, you can be quite individualistic.

You probably have a good mastery of the facts and skills essential in your field of work. You are logical and decisive. You willingly provide help to others when needed, but rebel against requirements which do not make sense to you.

You can be counted on to keep track of facts and details and to get the job done on schedule. You work best when there is structure and order and some privacy for concentration. You like to see tangible results and cost savings if possible.

With your good organizational skills and strong commitment to meeting deadlines, time management is probably not a problem for you. Some ISTJs have mentioned getting bogged down with small details, sometimes getting overloaded due to accepting more responsibility than they could handle, and having difficulty delegating tasks to those who do not share their workstyle; however, most ISTJs really do seem to have it together as far as time management is concerned. They get things done and they simply don't miss deadlines.

I asked six ISTJs how they deal with time management. These ISTJs are not necessarily typical of their types, but their stories can provide helpful information for you and others. Several identify how they make the most of the strengths which result from their type preferences. Unlike most other personality types, they did not offer many suggestions to others of their type, because they felt such advice would not be needed. However, they did offer a few useful ideas.

Stories, Ideas, & Suggestions

Brenda

Q. Tell me about an occasion when you felt really successful in managing your time.

My third year at University was a particularly exceptional example of my time management excellence! I had a full course load, was working 30 hours per week managing a swimming pool and had a boyfriend in another city. Most of my courses had fairly lengthy term papers as part of the course requirements so I knew I'd need to be very strict with my time. So... I created a schedule for each semester, outlining what days I would be researching specific papers, when I should be in the 'writing' phase, and when I would be typing - working backward from the deadlines and allowing for times when I'd have to be studying for mid-terms! I also allotted reading time to keep up with the course so I wouldn't have to 'cram' for mid-terms. I had a folder system for each paper. (I think I had eight to do in a four month time-frame) and began researching topics during the very first week of class. So in fact, I was in 'research' phase for multiple papers at the same time... I just kept to my schedule and would stop working on Abnormal Psych at 2:00 p.m. and move on to Social Psych... etc. etc. Eventually, I ended up having to pay someone to type my last few papers because it was taking more time than I thought... but that was pretty well the only adjustment I had to make.

My reading schedule was even better! I would first read the selected chapters, then re-read with a halite pen and then make chapter summary notes! (Sometimes, I wouldn't get to phase three summary notes until just prior to the mid-term).

To keep my pool running smoothly I set the schedule for all the staff immediately, and lined up replacements for myself for the days when I knew I'd have to study for mid-terms and when I'd be going away to visit my boyfriend.

This is now 14 years ago, but I still consider that to be the most challenging scheduling exercise of my life!

Of course, I could tell you about when I was planning for my wedding and the little project plan I drew up for my husband and I... assigning tasks and deadlines... that was another good time too!

Q. Tell me about some of your difficulties in time management.

I really don't think I have any time management problems. I am very deadline driven and can quickly assess what steps I need to take in order to stay within the allowable time-frame. If I have too many things to do at one time, I usually eliminate some of them... or delegate. I have to admit though that when this happens, before I come to the conclusion that I must let some go or delegate, it causes me a lot of stress.

Q. What advice can you offer to others of your type regarding time management?

No advice for others of my type. Lots of advice for other types... but you didn't ask for that!

Roy

I don't mind sharing some of my insights with you. I think I've always been fairly adept at time management. Even in Kindergarten through grade 12, I'd look at the requirements I was facing, and work up a plan and schedule to accomplish the tasks I had listed. I've always kept lists. Almost always have beat deadlines.

Q. Tell me about an occasion when you felt really successful in managing your time.

One occasion which sticks out in my mind as being really successful, because of the financial impact/savings involved happened when I was working as an Instrument Engineer with power and light at a large nuclear power plant. I had inherited the radiation monitoring system on UNIT 2 right after start-up. The engineer who had oversight on the system during start-up had not seen to it that four high range monitors inside the containment building were calibrated according to the NRC guidelines/

regulations. This situation was one that the NRC really frowned upon and would levy a stiff fine for noncompliance.

I developed a plan to rotate the detectors out of containment and return them to the OEM for appropriate calibration. My plan entailed no loss of generation, absolute minimum exposure to the technicians who had to R&R the detectors, and speedy routing to the factory.

The NRC, through an audit, determined that we were in noncompliance, but because of the actions I had already taken, the time-table I had worked out, and the turn-a-round I had established with the factory, declined fining my company. Had they pursued a fine, it would have been in the 20 million dollar range, plus a substantial loss of generation through a shutdown period.

Because of the personal irritation experienced due to lack of planning/time management, I have disciplined myself to such a degree that I don't feel I have any significant difficulties in that area.

I would suspect that others with similar personalities/psychological type, would be as efficient, due to their drive for orderliness.

Sally

Q. Tell me about an occasion when you felt really successful in managing your time.

I always feel successful in managing my time.

Q. Tell me about some of your difficulties in time management.

I have no difficulties.

Q. What advice can you offer to others of your type regarding time management?

I can't imagine that other ISTJ's would need help in this regard, but if I had to give advice, it would be 'FOCUS'.

Q. What help would you like to get regarding time management from others of your type?

None.

Lisa

Q. Tell me about an occasion when you felt really successful in managing your time.

This is difficult to answer because I tend to focus on what DOESN'T get done, rather than what does. However, I do love it 'when a plan comes together.' I can't name a specific occasion when I remember 'time management' working like clockwork, my recollections are more around completed projects at the end of a long line that are on time (and preferably under-budget).

Q. Tell me about some of your difficulties in time management.

As a supervisor and someone who answers to those higher in the company and volunteer leaders in the organization, my time is very often not my own to dictate. Plans to complete a task at a specific time are often thwarted by projects/requests seen as more pressing by those requesting them.

Q. What advice can you offer to others of your type regarding time management?

For heaven's sake, save your sanity and try to 'go with the flow.' There's a book out, *'Don't Sweat the Small Stuff — And It's All Small Stuff.'* ISTJs could probably take a lesson from that. Learn to know what is CRITICAL, and don't think or behave as though every small decision is a monumental one.

Q. What help would you like to get regarding time management from others of your type?

How to squeeze even more out of a day? I'm on a constant quest to be even more productive, and appreciate any assistance in getting there! — Advice on how to relax might be good too, especially if you could show me how relaxation might, in the long-term scheme of things, improve productivity through better mental health! (less worry!)

Carole

Hi! Here it goes!

Q. Tell me about an occasion when you felt really successful in managing your time.

I have always been very able to manage my time. Although as an adult I write a 'to do' list on paper, it is always running in the background of my brain - like Windows 95. I can call it up at will. In fact, sometimes it is hard to escape it.

Since teen years on, I have known that if I truly wanted something I had only to focus on the goal, decide what I needed to do to achieve it and persevere. I grew up in a family who believed that 'the impossible takes a little bit longer'. This proverb was truly double-edged since I came to believe that there was no excuse for failure in reaching your goals.

Q. Tell me about some of your difficulties in time management.

Difficulties occur when I overextend myself and truly take on more than can fit into a 24 hour time period.

Q. What advice can you offer to others of your type regarding time management?

When the above situation occurs I need to add a column to my 'to do list' which indicates how much time is required to complete the task. This extra step brings home that I have set myself up for 'mission impossible'. With mission impossible comes, of course, a sense of failure. The latter is true if I believe I am not meeting my own image of who I am and what I can do. It's a very destructive phase to be caught in.

Q. What help would you like to get regarding time management from others of your type?

Other types have tried to tell me to 'slow down' — especially my ENFP spouse. However, it needs to be an internal re-adjustment.

Sharron

Q. Tell me about an occasion when you felt really successful in managing your time.

I feel managing my time best when I am able to know what tasks I have to do and I am able to work on them without interruption and to completion. I am currently working on a project that is really more organizational than anything else. It gives me a sense of accomplishment to keep it organized and flowing smoothly. But to do that, I need to wait till most people have finished their portion of the process and then I go through all of it every night and redistribute projects for the next day. It's working well, but I wonder if I'm obsessing about being organized?

Today I had multiple tasks to accomplish and I made a list the night before of all that needed to be done. When I arrived at work, I simply began down my list and crossed off the projects when they were completed. I find that when I get interrupted, I would just change my focus for that period of time and then get right back to my original project (even if further follow-up was needed on the interrupting project). I tend to be very methodical, but am also one of the only managers in my office that can be counted on to continually finish multiple tasks.

Q. Tell me about some of your difficulties in time management.

I get very frustrated with things that are beyond my control. When I have to delegate work and wait for others to get it done, I tend to get aggravated. I also have difficulties managing my time and projects when my work environment is not organized. If I have papers all over my desk, I have a hard time seeing past that to get the work done. I also have a hard time managing people who don't work the same way I do. It's very difficult when I have to manage someone who can't keep track of their projects and 'to do's'. I also had a very hard time working for someone who wasn't organized. Everything was done at the last minute and was always a crisis. I hated that and will never work for that type of person again (unless it's by accident).

Q. What advice can you offer to others of your type regarding time management?

I think the thing that helps me the most is getting myself organized for the next day before I leave work in the evening. When I have my priorities for the day organized, it makes it much easier to get right to it when I arrive at the office. Also, taking the time to organize your projects and prioritize them. Sometimes I feel like I spend too much time organizing myself, but I know that if I just try to remember everything I will not be as effective.

Q. What help would you like to get regarding time management from others of your type?

Tricks they use that help them be more efficient. How they are effective working with others (or managing others) who are not their type and do not like to make lists, prioritize, set deadlines, etc?

Discussion

Although all of the contributors said they were successful with managing time, some of them shared two common difficulties: a frustration with others who seem less organized, and a tendency to sometimes take on too much work.

With a clear inner sense of reality, supported by their logic, and driven by a strong desire to see tangible results, ISTJs are able to get things organized and done with great efficiency. For ISTJs, good time management is an integral part of their life's purpose.

Since efficient accomplishment is so important to their lives, it is logical that they would be successful time managers. They can be very frustrated with others who do not share their workstyle because they are so intent on getting things done and not missing deadlines.

The contributors to this study understood this. When asked to provide suggestions for others like themselves, most said they could not imagine an ISTJ having difficulty with time management. No advice seemed needed to improve the efficient ISTJ workstyle, although two people wanted more tips to help them be even more productive.

Most of the suggestions had to do with coping with other people who have different work-styles: "Remember that sometimes, to save your sanity, it is necessary to just try to 'go with the flow'." "Don't 'sweat the small stuff'. Read the book by this title. You'll find helpful hints about how to reduce stress on the job and in everyday life." "Try to find ways to relax; remember that in the long run, better mental health improves productivity." "Try not to worry so much when you have to delegate to others. "Try to recognise that others may be able to do the job satisfactorily even if their workstyle is different from yours."

Other suggestions had to do with not taking on too much work, and reducing stress: "Learn what is critical, and don't think or behave as though every small decision is necessarily a monumental one." "If you happen to overextend yourself and truly take on more than can fit into a 24 hour time period, try adding a column to your 'to do list' which indicates how much time is required to complete the task. This may enable you to realize that you have taken on too much, and help you to avoid being too hard on yourself if you can't do it all."

As mentioned earlier, type should not be an excuse for behaviour. Rather, an understanding of a person's natural preferences can be helpful in the development of an effective style which embraces whatever provides the driving force and gives life its meaning. ISTJs don't need many suggestions to improve their time management, but some contributors were able to offer a few useful ideas.

Helping ISTJs Find their Own Way

Characteristics and behaviours which could be expected of an ISTJ

- hard working

- practical

- systematic

- thorough in approach to tasks

- like to have a good mastery of the essential facts

- logical

- decisive

- willing to provide help to others when needed

- rebel against requirements which do not make sense

- good at keeping track of details

- like to get the job done on schedule

- appreciate structure and order

- like some privacy for concentration

- like to see tangible results

- like to make cost savings if possible

Driving forces
To get things done efficiently.

Problems *most* likely to occur
Frustration with others who have different work-styles. Sometimes take on too much work.

Solutions *least* likely to be followed
Just go with the flow.

Suggestions

Here are a few ideas which may help reduce stress.

1. Don't 'sweat the small stuff.'

- Read the book by this title. (It's included in the reference section). You'll find helpful hints about how to reduce stress on the job and in everyday life.

- Remember that sometimes, to save your sanity, you really do have to 'go with the flow.'

- Learn what is critical, and don't think or behave as though every small decision is necessarily a monumental one.

- Try to find ways to relax; remember that in the long run, better mental health improves productivity.

2. Find ways to delegate.

- Try not to worry so much when you have to delegate to others. Try to recognise that others may be able to do the job satisfactorily even if their workstyle is different from yours.

- If you happen to overextend yourself and truly take on more than can fit into a 24 hour time period, try adding a column to your 'to do list' which indicates how much time is required to complete the task. This may enable you to realize that you have taken on too much, and help you to avoid being too hard on yourself if you can't do it at all.

3. Keep doing what you do well!

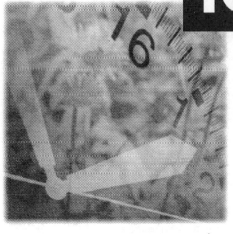

Chapter | *16*

ISTP

An Introduction to ISTP

If you are an ISTP, you are probably cheerful and optimistic and likely to trust that everything will turn out well in the end. You have a natural bent for hands-on or technical things.

You are energetic and enjoy situations where there are lots of opportunities for action, freedom, and excitement. You hate to be tied down to conventional systems or boring routines with too much talk and not enough action. You believe people should be respected, not for their rank or academic degree, but for their ability to put out on the job. You resist taking orders from people who don't seem to know what they are doing. You believe rules are meant to be broken if you can find a better way.

At work, you want to do the job as quickly as possible. You tend to 'go with the flow,' using your skills to make contributions as problems arise. You will frequently drop what you are doing in order to help with something urgent which has come up. In order to save time, you like to find ways to take short-cuts. If others do not understand what you are doing, they may think your work is incomplete or that your approach is haphazard. You may sometimes be accused of quitting too soon, giving up and moving on to something else.

I asked five ISTPs how they try to cope with time management. It was not easy to get ISTPs to answer some of my questions because most ISTPs were resistant to talking about time management 'difficulties' or 'weaknesses.' As one participant commented, "some people experience time very differently than others with the current fashion of time management being just one in ascendency..." The five ISTPs who responded are not necessarily typical of their type, but their stories can provide helpful insights and information for you and others.

Stories, Ideas, & Suggestions

John

Q. Tell me about an occasion when you felt really successful in managing your time.

I have never felt this. Well perhaps for five minutes after I went to a TMI course.

On the other hand, I rarely, if ever, miss deadlines. Things get done when they need to get done.

Q. Tell me about some of your difficulties in time management.

The assumption underlying this is that time is something that needs to be managed. If this is the case then there will, almost by definition, be 'difficulties.' But if time is something to be experienced then the difficulty becomes one of "what could I be missing out because there are too many demands on me right now?"

Q. What advice can you offer to others of your type regarding time management?

Experience the current moment to the fullest you can. Work, play, relax, and let the future take care of itself.

Q. What help would you like to get regarding time management from others of your type?

Not help, just to hear how they relate to the moment.

Kevin

I thought I'd offer you a bit of discussion on this from my perspective. I'll mix in citation snippets from your mail along with a little general rambling; good luck pulling anything useful out of it.

By way of background and disclaimers, I am a 39 year old engineer. I make no claims for other ISTPs and I seem to be rather a-typical in many ways if the type descriptions in the MBTI books are anything to go by. (Neither am I very INTP by the descriptions in those same books).

We know that some types find time management easier than others, but we all have to solve our time management problems somehow.

This 'paradigm' (an overused word) is a foreign one to me, and I expect to ISTPs in general. I understand what is meant by it, but it really doesn't apply to me. Time isn't something to be 'managed', it's something to experience - to flow through and with. My approach to time is to make sure I have lots of uncommitted blocks of it to simply live in - do whatever seems interesting at the time, including 'nothing'. So I guess my management of time is to make sure I have lots of free time.

Ten years ago, or so, when time management became a major focus of the business world and of all shakers and movers with goals and such, our company introduced Franklin Day Planners as company issue material, had courses on time management, etc. It took four or five years of me politely declining a Planner before the secretaries finally stopped asking me for my order in November for the upcoming year's Planner contents and options. I was apparently the only person in our engineering group of some 35 people who did this and they could not understand me. To this day I'm sure I'm an enigma to them.

In spite of my oddity in this matter, I am a highly valued employee, senior engineer, etc. My approach to time 'management' is best described as battlefield triage. The cases that are hopeless you let die, the ones who aren't too bad off you give anaesthetic and store somewhere for later, those needing serious treatment and standing a good chance of benefiting from it get the immediate attention.

Q. Tell me about an occasion when you felt really successful in managing your time.

My stance is this: if I have to write down things that are important, my life is too busy. If I have to manage time in the usual sense of the word, my life needs adjustment. I felt most successful at time management when I started closing down the too many commitments I'd allowed to gather over the first part of my life so I was feeling frazzled. In retrospect this marked the onset of my midlife crisis ('transition' to use the kinder, gentler phrase). Of course the level of commitments I had were trivial compared to what most people concerned with time management juggle, but they were more than I was psychologically able to be deal with.

Now, at home and work, I have a calendar. Just a standard one with about inch square spaces per day to write something in. The few things that are important which I might not or won't remember (like, say, a dentist appointment made six months in advance) I write down. A meeting at work - I write down. Everything else I either remember (and I have a poor memory) or it simply isn't important enough for me to bother with. Going back through past months this year, I have 3-5 items per month written down. This strategy has been successful for me.

Q. Tell me about some of your difficulties in time management.

The only difficulties I consider difficulties is when I over-commit. I'm much better at not getting into that situation now. Of course there are lots of people who consider me to have numerous time management difficulties because they don't share my life values and priorities. Learning how to deal with such people gracefully and understanding where they and I differ was helpful.

To be sure there are many people who would suggest I have 'a time management problem,' just as there are people who think I have political, religious, and what have you, problems because my views and actions are different from theirs. But my style doesn't prevent me from being very valued at work, and I am always punctual when I commit to something of my own will. The stuff that needs to get done, gets done, the make-work is optional, self-imposed deadlines are forgotten...

Q. What advice can you offer to others of your type regarding time management?

Nothing comes to mind. I don't expect I track most ISTPs and they really wouldn't care about my personal life story anyway.

Q. What help would you like to get regarding time management from others of your type?

Nothing comes to mind.

Dave

Here are some thoughts I had regarding your questionnaire.

My successes:

When I was in sales with a former company, time management was very important as many balls could be in the air at one time. I felt successful when I could meet all my appointments, deadlines, duties and personal commitments on time and complete. I hated to have things hanging over my head.

My difficulties:

Procrastinating on things I don't like to do till they become more of an emergency or a bigger problem.

Advice to other ISTPs:

- Get your priorities in order and plan. Then work your plan.

- Avoid doing everything you like first and leaving the other tasks you don't like to the end.

- Be flexible so as to switch tasks if something changes. Don't procrastinate or at least be aware you tend to put things off and compensate for that.

- A friendly reminder or a gentle push is sometimes all we need to set the world on fire.

Frank

Q. Tell me about an occasion when you felt really successful in managing your time.

This occasion... I filled this out while driving over.

Q. Tell me about some of your difficulties in time management.

Balancing family and customer demands.

Q. What advice regarding time management could you offer to others of your type?

When you commit to doing something, and say when you'll have it done, don't overestimate your abilities.

Irvin

Q. Tell me about an occasion when you felt really successful in managing your time.

Getting our flyer produced in time. We didn't think we'd get it out in time, but it was important, and everyone worked hard, and somehow it got done.

Q. Tell me about some of your difficulties in time management.

- Phone interruptions (especially with the cell phone).

- Not writing down a list of things to do.

- Having to deal with other people's problems.

Q. What advice regarding time management could you offer to others of your type?

- Do what you know is important.

- Make a list if there are many things to remember.

- Try not to let phone interruptions interfere with your work. Kill the cell phone for a while.

Discussion

Most of the ISTP contributors did not seem very concerned with time management. They got the urgent things done and they were satisfied with that. Some seemed annoyed with others who 'got on their backs' about planning ahead.

This was not surprising. According to type theory, the force that animates ISTPs is the inner need to analyze the world, not to run it. With the sensing auxiliary, this takes a hands-on or practical form. ISTPs feel driven to respond to situations which require immediate attention. Otherwise they are not much interested.

When asked to provide suggestions for others like themselves, the ISTP contributors offered only ideas which would enable ISTPs to be themselves while somehow meeting the demands of the workplace.

The suggestions were mostly practical: "Try not to procrastinate, or at least be aware that you tend to put things off, and compensate for that." "Don't overestimate your abilities when committing to how long something is going to take." "Make a list if there are many things to remember."

ISTPs do not like to plan, but these ISTPs know that some sort of prioritizing and planning may be necessary. "Avoid doing everything you like first and leaving other tasks you don't like to the end." "Try to get your priorities in order and try to make a plan, then work your plan." The plan would be just a rough one, however, with room to deal with the urgent demands or pleasures of the moment.

To help deal with others who might get on your back, there was this suggestion: "Try to learn to deal gracefully with people who don't share your life values." "Try not to let the phone interfere with your work. Kill the cell phone for a while."

As mentioned earlier, type should not be an excuse for behaviour. Rather, an understanding of a person's natural preferences can be helpful in the development of an effective style which embraces whatever provides the driving force and gives life its joy. The contributors, by recognizing what is important in their own lives, were able to offer some useful suggestions to help ISTPs.

Helping ISTPs Find their Own Way

Characteristics and behaviours which could be expected of an ISTP

- generally cheerful

- optimistic

- like hands-on or technical things

- energetic

- like action

- appreciate freedom

- want excitement

- hate to be tied down to boring routines

- respect people's ability to put out on the job

- resist taking orders from people who don't seem to know what they are doing

- believe rules can to be broken if there is a better way

- want to do the job as quickly as possible

- tend to 'go with the flow'

- deal with problems as they arise

- always willing to help with something urgent

- like to find short-cuts

Driving forces
To go with the flow, do what's necessary when it's necessary.

Problems *most* likely to occur
Not appearing to take their work seriously.

Solutions *least* likely to be followed
Follow a schedule.

Suggestions

Here are a few suggestions to enable you to be yourself while meeting the minimum demands of the workplace.

1. Improve your reliability.

- Do what you know is important.

- Try to get your priorities in order and try to make a plan, then work your plan.

- Make a list if there are many things to remember.

- Avoid doing everything you like first and leaving other tasks you don't like to the end.

- Try not to procrastinate, or at least be aware that you tend to put things off, and compensate for that.

- Don't over-commit; don't overestimate your abilities when estimating to how long something is going to take.

- Try not to let the phone interfere with your work. Kill the cell phone sometimes.

2. Build on your ability to respond to the moment.

- Experience the current moment to the fullest you can.

- Be flexible so you can switch tasks if something changes.

3. Try to learn to deal gracefully with people who don't share your life values.

Type & Time Management

Comparisons, Contrasts, Questions, and Conclusions

Reflections

As I read the time management stories from all the contributors, I could not help but feel that people of my own type (INFP) have the biggest challenges with regard to time management. We INFPs want to live in harmony, and we want everyone else in our circle to live in harmony too; so whatever we do, we feel we must make sure that everyone is comfortable and satisfied. At the same time, we feel we must keep altering and improving our work, to make sure that everything is not only correct but also balanced and consistent with our values. The result must feel right, and it must fit in with the whole context of our lives, which are constantly changing. No wonder we delay starting some projects because we know they will become so complicated and will absorb so much of our time and concentration.

Yet it is my husband (an ENTJ) who seems to be the busiest! He has time management challenges too, because he is so compelled to take responsibility, make decisions, and get things done. It's a heavy load, and it's especially hard because he believes in work before play, and the work is never done. He has so many ideas and wants to get involved in so many activities, that there is always one more thing to take responsibility for. He actually has to schedule time for play. From my perspective, when 'play' is scheduled, it's not so much fun any more.

Of course, my friend, Shirley, would say it is the ENFJs who have a hard time, because they feel they must not only get things done on time, they must also meet the needs of the people around them. Life is a continual balancing act for them.

If you read all of the stories, you will have noticed that each group of people have a different set of difficulties which arise because of their natural preferences. How people tend to deal with these difficulties (or whether they perceive them as difficulties at all) depends on their natural preferences also. People who have studied personality theory will notice how expected behaviours and characteristics were exemplified in some of the stories. They will also find many examples of diversity within each type. It is not surprising that people with different preferences need different time management styles.

There are many dramatic contrasts in the ways people of different personality types deal with time management. The differences between people with Judging and Perceiving preferences are probably the most noticeable. There are also many examples of how the Feeling preference has an effect on people's time management needs. The effects of the Intuiting and Sensing preferences can also be noted.

The time management stories also give rise to many intriguing issues and questions. What are the differences in the need for control among the different personality types and how is this related to time management style? What are some contrasts and comparisons in the ways different personality types experience creativity or personal satisfaction in their work? How do 'time management requirements' affect the physical or emotional health of different kinds of people? These issues and questions may be especially interesting to you if you are an 'N' type. You may find that this is just the beginning of further ideas you would like to explore. If you are a researcher, you may use some of the questions or issues which emerged to form hypotheses for further research.

This section will begin to explore a few of the interesting contrasts, comparisons, questions, and issues which emerged from the stories.

Comparisons and Contrasts

Judging or Perceiving Preferences

People with a preference for Judging usually 'plan their work and work their plan.' They like making decisions quickly, and they appreciate having matters settled. People with a perceiving preference enjoy gathering information. They are usually very flexible and can respond to the spontaneous moment. Just for fun, compare these excerpts from the stories. Each pair is the same except for the Judging or Perceiving preference. Notice how these preferences affect time management issues.

ENFJ/ENFP

Mostly, I try to accomplish an awful lot every day. I am a business owner, mother of two, homeowner, spouse, child and sister. It is an awful lot to juggle. Prioritizing and scheduling are the only ways I keep sane.

—Karen, ENFJ

I rely on my instincts and last minute 'aha' moments to get me through to conclusion on a project. With my experience of coming up with what I need in time (albeit JUST in time) , I continue to expect success. And it usually comes.

—Peg, ENFP

ENTJ/ENTP

I get very frustrated when I lag behind or miss deadlines. It drives me nuts to be late on a deadline, and frankly, I get embarrassed about it.

—Gayla, ENTJ

I have no problem making myself late. I usually tell myself that if someone else is going to be mad, then they'll be mad. Oh well. I am never really successful in managing my time.

—Steve, ENTP

ESFJ/ESFP

I found the best way to focus my energies was to develop a check list of every task, some very basic, that needed to be completed and the date by which it needed to be completed. This helped me to stay focused on priorities and ensure that nothing was overlooked.

—Ann, ESFJ

I tend to put things off and do them closer to their due date. Next year is another millennium for me and I will worry about those items later. This creates some stress in those that like to see work completed on a programmed schedule.

—John, ESFP

ESTJ/ESTP

I do not have a lot of difficulties in managing my time. I've always planned ahead and most of the time. It works well.

—Andre, ESTJ

...I often forget my schedule for the next day unless there's something crucially important. And I don't find many things crucially important.

—Newman, ESTP

INFJ/INFP

Difficulties almost invariably relate to letting myself get overwhelmed and/or anxious about how I'm going to get it all done.

—Mary, INFJ

I pick and choose these projects and am usually quite able to say no if I feel I cannot give my all to it.

—Sherril, INFP

INTJ/INTP

I'm a planner so I usually know how I'm going to spend my time and I budget my time in advance.

—Gayla, INTJ

I very much like to go with the flow, doing tasks as they appeal to me.

—Sandy, INTP

ISFJ/ISFP

I make lists and more lists and then I feel good when I scratch something off as DONE! ...To me everything on my list is important. .

-Jerry, ISFJ

I usually don't have any structure—I just kind of know what to do and eventually do it.

—D.C., ISFP

ISTJ/ISTP

I really don't think I have any time management problems. I am very deadline driven and can quickly assess what steps I need to take in order to stay within the allowable timeframe.

—Brenda, ISTJ

The stuff that needs to get done, gets done, the make-work is optional, self-imposed deadlines are forgotten...

—Kevin, ISTP

Sensing and Intuiting Preferences

People with a Sensing preference tend to take in information through the five senses. They appreciate using accurate, detailed, factual information to deal with the here and now.

People with an Intuitive preference use insights, associations, and connections. They use ideas and imagination, and they consider insights and analogies to generalize and anticipate the future.

The Intuitives seem to have a more time-consuming job on their hands (or rather, in their minds!) at the beginning stages of the project. People with Sensing preferences feel comfortable getting right down to the job, but the Intuitives want to spend more time working on the big picture before they start. Many intuitive contributors talk about feeling overwhelmed, perhaps because they see so many possibilities, and all these take time to consider. Once the project has begun, the Intuitives continue to be tempted by a multitude of new ideas and possibilities in the world around them. One 'NJ' said: "My 'N' fights my 'J', and my 'N' usually wins!"

For some of the 'NP' types, giving in to temptations and distractions sometimes seems part of the fun of living (although it does create problems which have to be solved). But for the 'NJs' it was a battle which some believed they had to push themselves to win. As one INFJ put it: "...pushing myself unrealistically results in failure of closure and at the same time I have been forcing the beautiful balance of the outer world..."

Compare the different ways these people approach or manage a project:

ENFJ/ESFJ

I have to truly understand the big picture... I let my head rule the planner and let the planner be my reminder not my dictator.

—Deb , ENFJ

I find myself always wanting to do little detail jobs first while I ponder about the bigger projects as I am doing the little pieces. I find I need to work on those little pieces to eventually come to the big project with enough concrete pieces to see a big pattern and picture.

—Martha, ESFJ

ENTJ/ESTJ

I usually manage all of my activities by never putting anything away. Piles are growing all over my house and office. The minute I try to organize the stuff, I can't find anything.

—M.E., ENTJ

The best way to manage our time is to be well organized in what we do. Get rid of unnecessary stuff and concentrate on important things. I manage to place/store whatever I'm working with the minute I'm finished using it. This way, should I need to work with it later on, I don't lose time in searching for it. For example, my files are always up to date and stored at the right place. Should I or somebody else need information, I'm ready. Once everything is stored away you find yourself with more time to do other stuff.

—Andre , ESTJ

ENFP/ESFP

My style is, now, to prepare ahead, or at least to think about a project well before it is due and let it simmer. Then, when it is actually nearing the due date, I tend to do what is necessary in a fairly quick burst of activity.

—Robert, ENFP

I can do the long range projects but they are not my first choice. I do well with 'attention to detail' activities...

—John, ESFP

ENTP/ESTP

I'm great at managing my time when I have a big, team-oriented, intellectual project I can really sink my teeth into. ... I love to see the streams come together. I find this role extremely motivating. It's exactly what I want to do, so of course I have no trouble managing my time. I'm able to map out general plans, e.g., a monthly timeline, and get the buy-in of others.

—Hal, ENTP

Simplify and be happy.

—Newman, ESTP

Feeling or Thinking Preferences

The Feeling or Thinking preferences have to do with the way we make decisions or categorize information. People with a Thinking preference tend to prefer an analytical, objective approach. People with a Feeling preference like to consider the impact of the decision on their own values, their own feelings, and those of others in their family or workplace. Thinkers want a logical outcome; Feelers want a harmonious outcome. These preferences have an impact on how people choose to spend their time, and on how long it takes to make decisions and move on to the next task. People with a Feeling preference sometimes need more time because it takes longer to gather and sift through personal information and to consider the effects of the decision on other people. People with a Feeling preference also tend to be distracted from the task at hand by their personal desire to respond to other people's needs. Responding to people's needs can be very time consuming. (Have you ever tried to rock a baby fast? Comfort a child quickly?)

But the Feeling preference could also improve efficiency in some cases by helping to motivate people who tend to procrastinate, but do not wish to 'let others down.'

Consider some of these quotations from Feeling types:

My difficulties in time management are that I am easily distracted by people issues. If I have to choose between task and people I will do the people process first. However, because of Puritan work ethic, stubbornness, pride... I will complete the task on time even if it means giving up sleep or recreation time.

—Doug, ENFJ

...with my tendency to make people happy, and to put things off until I'm 'inspired', I can often get caught in a jam...

—Peg, ENFP

Main difficulty is that I take on too much. I tend to believe that I can do anything and because I enjoy helping others I will agree to give them my time to finish their projects.

—Janet, ESFJ

...I don't like to fall short of a commitment or let people down so I'll use this to help myself perform better.

—Bruce, ESFP

If I have difficulty in time management it's when I have too much to juggle. This occurs most often in trying to juggle my home responsibilities and my workload. It gets so overwhelming that I go blank in what and how things should be prioritized.

—Julie, ISFJ

...I was working full-time, enrolled in a weekend college program working on my bachelor's degree... all the while caring for a family (husband and three small children...). I look back on it and wonder how I did it. According to my husband, he didn't suffer. According to my children, they did not suffer. I was tired but focused...

—Karen, INFJ

I am easily distracted by the needs of others, and in general I say 'yes' to too many requests, which interfere with my own private preparation time.

—Sarah, INFP

I often find it more difficult to manage time when I am the sole beneficiary of the task, whereas I can readily get things done for others who I care about.

—Bob, ISFP

Although people with Thinking preferences also take time to help others, generally they do not express a heartfelt desire to interrupt their current activities in order to respond to someone else's needs unless they are convinced it is necessary.

Interruptions seemed to be an annoyance, particularly for those people with both a Thinking and a Judging Preference who try hard to keep on task and get the job done.

I tend to forget to allow for roadblocks caused by things and people over which I have no control.

—Linda, ENTJ

Time management is most difficult when I am bombarded with constant interruptions by other staff...

—William, ESTJ

Difficulties occur when plans to complete a task at a specific time are thwarted by projects/requests seen as more pressing by those requesting them.

—Lisa, ISTJ

Advice for others: Call when you know you won't reach a talkative person and leave a specific voice mail or answering machine message. Saves a lot of time in some instances.

—Stan, INTJ

For Thinking types with a Perceiving preference, interruptions or diversions could be seen as an excuse to stop working on a current task, but only if the diversion is interesting or fun.

...my time-wasting ways - interesting but irrelevant conversations, speculations, humour, competition, moodiness

—Hal, ENTP

I'm creative and love to chase new concepts/ activities/adventures. Doing this, I lose myself and sense of time.

—Darlene, INTP

Some people with a Thinking preference may take a logical approach when deciding whether to respond to the demands of others.

My approach to time management is best described as a battlefield triage. The cases that are hopeless you let die, the ones who aren't too bad off you give anaesthetic and store somewhere for later, those needing serious treatment and standing a good chance of benefiting from it get the immediate attention.

—Kevin, ISTP

These are just some of the contrasts that can be considered by studying the stories and ideas offered by people of different personality types. From these contrasts, it is apparent that people with different preferences frequently face different problems concerning time management. They need different time management systems because they have different needs. The reference section includes the names of some other books which can deepen your understanding of personality type differences.

Questions

Time and Control

Today, in the modern western world, who or what is in control of our time? When people say they 'manage' their time well, are they really the ones in control? Or are they just operating comfortably under the current system, whatever it happens to be?

Compare these excerpts from the stories. Who (or what?) is the controlling force?

Once the schedule is set, it rules my time with the class, barring special opportunities or more interest than anticipated in a topic. The students receive this course calendar on the first day of classes. It is a kind of contract between us as to what I will provide and what will be expected of them. No debate here. It gives me a sense of control. I know where I am going and so do those most directly affected.

—Marvin, ENTJ

I want to have a sense of control, primarily over myself rather than others because personal competence is important (or at least the appearance of competence). I need a sense of order and direction, and purpose. My need to manage time would be primarily to achieve personal goals and objectives, and more so if these goals are connected to something larger than myself...

—Jerrold, ENTJ

If I have difficulty in time management it's when I have too much to juggle. This occurs most often in trying to juggle my home responsibilities and my workload. It gets so overwhelming that I go blank in what and how things should be prioritized.

—Julie, ISFJ

Once I begin, a project takes on a life of its own.

—Pat, INFP

In the first excerpt, Marvin feels in control, but it is really he who is being controlled by the system or schedule. In the second, Jerrold wants to have a sense of control, recognizing that the his goals are connected to something larger than himself. In the third excerpt, Julie wants control, but is overwhelmed by the need to meet opposing demands from different sources which wield control over her life. In the fourth example, Pat has relinquished control, giving it over to the project itself.

So, managing our time can give us opportunities to become masters or slaves... or to feel like we are masters or slaves. Ironically, we can even become slaves to whatever devices we use to become better masters, an idea which is suggested in the next excerpt:

...In this ever busier world we live in we have created many devices that are supposed to save us time, with the inherent assumption that we will have more time to do 'useful and productive things'... with all these electronic marvels we can now allow others to make instant demands on our time so that they, in practice, manage our time for us. I really think the concept that we can effectively manage our time is a myth...
—Terry, INTP

For some personality types, such as INFPs, relinquishing control to the project itself can be a desirable thing, encouraging the creative drive. For others, such as ENTJs, the person needs to think they are in control. In this way, personality type seems to affect the degree to which people think they must manage their time and the effort they make to do so. This would be a fascinating topic for further exploration.

Creativity and Personal Satisfaction

People with certain preferences seem to need to manage their time differently than others, in order to experience creativity and personal satisfaction. This suggests that such time management approaches as 'planning the work and working the plan' may be counterproductive for some people, especially those with Perceiving preferences.

Consider these excerpts:

I thrive on the last minute crunch that may look like we'll never make it... and then, low and behold, the project comes through. It may finish at midnight, but it meets customer timelines, and exceeds expectations.

—Pat, ENFP

When I am interested in something, time has no meaning for me. I often become lost in new and exciting things that I find.

—Steve, ENTP

I very much like to go with the flow, doing tasks as they appeal to me. I only make lists when I have to remember something, but as helpful as it is to have a list or a reminder, I even balk at the effort it takes to pick up the paper and pencil to write something down most of the time. (Sadly, good ideas can fade away!)

—Sandy, INTP

I have struggled a lot with getting things done in advance, rather than being inspired and creative at the last minute. One of my difficulties is that SOMETIMES when I do manage to prepare in advance, I actually don't have the sparkle or creative energy to make the work good.

—Sarah, INFP

Working in a linear fashion (one thing at a time) may be counterproductive for some (but not necessarily all) people with Intuitive preferences.

Consider these examples:

It seems that I am most successful with my time management when I have multiple intriguing projects going at one time. The requirement to complete all the work on time - coupled with the excitement I have for the projects - allow me to focus on my work and organize tasks.

—Susan, ENFP

I think that I am most successful when I have the most to do.

—Melinda, ENFJ

Went to a remote location. Took all I needed to exist until project was completed and took a single project to work on.

—Stan, INTJ

I feel pretty successful at managing my time when my multitasking effectiveness (not necessarily raw efficiency) is high. That's when I'm in the 'zone,' making progress in a wide variety of areas, but it's all getting done effortlessly and, in fact, giving me energy .

—Kartik, ENTP

Physical or Emotional Health

People of almost every personality type tell stories of how their efforts to 'succeed' at time management cause stress or discomfort. However, if you look closely at the stories, you notice that there are differences in the kinds of circumstances which cause stress for different people.

Therefore, it makes sense that the solutions to their problems should be different also.

Consider these excerpts:

I am slowing down and taking time to smell the roses. I wish I was smarter earlier in life.

—Mary Ellen, ENTJ

I let myself get overwhelmed or anxious about how I am going to get it all done...

—Mary, INFJ

I often feel guilty and berate myself for not doing a better job of it.

—Leslie, ENFP

I have received all the help in the time management arena I wanted from my ex-wife. She tried her darnedest to get me to keep a pocket organizer and to be more punctual. It didn't work, though I felt guilty more...

—Newman, ESTP

There is a downside to the big picture time management. The positive is that it is more balanced for me (mind, body, emotion, spirit). The downside is that not as much gets done — and I often will feel that I am not doing enough.

—Jan , INFP

How to squeeze even more out of a day? I'm on a constant quest to be even more productive...

—Lisa, ISTJ

What could I be missing out because there are too many demands on me right now?

—John, ISTP

Things often take longer than I think they will so I get frustrated when there is less time left after the task is completed than I expected or when I don't accomplish what I set out to at the beginning of the day.

—Dianne, ENTP

I am easily sidetracked and find myself working on several tasks at one time. This causes frustration...

— David, ESFP

...I describe myself as time bound. I make lists and more lists... This is a curse. I am always checking my watch or a clock, everything is related to making use of a valuable resource, which of course is time...

—Jerry, ISFJ

I want a feeling of completion and am often afraid I won't get it done in the time I have...

—Sally, INTJ

I would say that the greatest difficulty in time management is that there are not enough hours in the day and I wish I didn't have to sleep.

—Janet, ESFJ

I get very stressed forcing myself to meet my scheduled appointments.

—Joanne, ENFJ

When I do things with procrastinators or people who change their minds too often, I have a problem...

—Andre, ESTJ

I really think we have an obsession with so called 'time management' to a point that has become pathological.

—Terry, INTP

I often leave things to the last minute and then work like a demon to get them done (if I have to).

—D.C., ISFP

Conclusions

It is fascinating to consider the dramatic contrasts, comparisons, and thought provoking questions which emerged from the sixteen collections of stories. But the heart of this book is the stories, ideas, and suggestions themselves. As we hear and appreciate each voice, we are reminded that we are all different, yet we are bonded with similarities too. Once we begin to understand ourselves, we can learn from others. We all have gifts and strengths for which we are valued; and we all have problems which we must solve in a way which is most effective for us. Although each individual must search for his or her own most effective way, others can help us by sharing their experiences and their ideas.

As explained in the introductory section, the collections of stories, ideas, and suggestions of each type were all sent back to the contributors for review and comment and to find out if the material seemed useful for each personality type. The comments were very affirming. People of each type found useful and interesting information. But the last word is yours.

You are invited to add your comments, your suggestions, your ideas and your personal stories to this thorny and unwieldy topic. The Readers' Invitation tells you how you can do this.

Readers' Invitation

We are already considering a next edition of this book, and you have an opportunity to contribute to it.

Here are three ways you may contribute:

1) You may answer the following four questions:

   i. Tell me about an occasion when you felt really successful in managing your time.

   ii. Tell me about some of your difficulties in time management.

   iii. What advice can you offer to others of your type regarding time management?

   iv. What help would you like to get regarding time management?

Remember to include your four-letter code as identified by the Myers-Briggs Personality Type Indicator.

2) You may offer comments on some of the stories, ideas, or suggestions which were presented in the chapter for your type.

3) You may suggest applications for using type for counselling or for time management workshops. You might like to try out some of your own ideas, and tell us how they worked out.

You may e-mail your ideas to sfitzsim@compusmart.ab.ca., you may fax them to (780) 469-2283. Attention: Sharon, or mail them to Psychometrics Canada Ltd., 7125-77 Avenue, Edmonton, AB, T6B 0B5, Canada.

References

Hirsh, Sandra, & Kise, Jane. *Work it Out: Clues for Solving People Problems at Work.* Palo Alto, CA: Davies-Black, 1996.

Hirsh, Sandra, & Kummerow, Jean. *Life Types: Understand Yourself and Make the Most of Who You Are.* NY: Warner Books, 1989.

Hirsh, Sandra K., & Kummerow, Jean M. *Introduction to Type in Organizations,* 3rd Ed. Palo Alto, CA: Consulting Psychologists Press, 1998.

Isachsen, Olaf, & Berens, Linda. *Working Together: A Personality-Centered Approach to Management,* 3rd ed. San Juan Capistrano, CA: Institute for Management Development, 1995.

Kroeger, Otto, & Thuesen, Janet. *Type Talk.* NY: Dell Publishing, 1988.

Kroeger, Otto, & Thuesen, Janet. *Type Talk at Work.* NY: Dell Publishing, 1992.

Hammer, Allen, Ed. MBTI Applications: *A Decade of Research on the Myers-Briggs Type Indicator.* CPP, 1996.

Lawrence, Gordon. *People Types and Tiger Stripes, 3rd Ed.* Gainesville, FL: Centre for Application of Psychological Type Inc., 1993.

Marsh, Bonnie. *Pumpkin Soup.* Gainesville, FL: Centre for Application of Psychological Type, 1984.

Myers, Isabel Briggs, & Myers, Peter. *Gifts Differing.* Palo Alto, CA: Consulting Psychologists Press, 1980.

Myers, Isabel Briggs, with revisions by Myers, K. & Kirby, L. *Introduction to Type. Fifth ed.* Palo Alto, CA: Consulting Psychologists Press, 1993.

Myers, Isabel Briggs, & McCaulley, M., Quenk, N., & Hammer, A. *Manual, 3rd Edition: A Guide to the Development and Use of the Myers-Briggs type Indicator.* Paul Alto, CA: Consulting Psychologists Press, 1998.

Pearman, Roger, & Albritton, Sarah. *I'm Not Crazy, I'm Just Not You.* Palo Alto, CA: Davies-Black, 1997.

Quenk, Naomi. *Beside Ourselves: Our Hidden Personality in Everyday Life.* Palo Alto, CA: Davies-Black Publishing, 1993.

Quenk, Naomi. *In the Grip: Our Hidden Personality.* Palo Alto, CA: Consulting Psychologists Press, 1996.

Thompson, Thomas, Ed. *Most Excellent Differences.* Gainesville, FL: Centre for Application of Psychological Type, 1996.

Books Mentioned by Some Participants

Carlson, Richard. *Don't Sweat the Small Stuff.* NY: Hyperion Books. 1998.

Covey, Stephen. *The Seven Habits of Highly Effective People.* NY: Fireside Books, reprint ed. 1990.

Covey, Stephen. *First Things First.* NY: Simon and Schuster, 1994.

Organizations Which Can Provide Further Information About the Myers-Briggs Type Indicator

Psychometrics Canada Ltd.
7125 - 77 Ave.
Edmonton, AB
Canada, T6B OB5
Tel: (780) 469 2268
Fax: (780) 469 2283
E-mail:info@psychometrics.com
Website: www.psychometrics.com

Association for Psychological Type
9140 Ward Parkway
Kansas City, MO 64144, U.S.A.
Tel: (816) 444 3500
Fax: (816) 444 0330
E-mail: staff@aptcentral.org
Website: www.aptcentral.org

**Centre for Applications of
Psychological Type**
2815 NW 13th Street, Suite 401
Gainesville, FL 32609, U.S.A.
Tel: (352) 375-0160
Fax: (352) 378-0503
E-mail: capt@capt.org
Website: www.capt.org

Consulting Psychologists Press, Inc.
3803 East Bayshore Road, U.S.A.
P.O. Box 10096
Palo Alto, CA 94303
Tel: (415) 969 8901
Fax: (415) 969 8608
E-mail: perms@cpp-db.com
Website: www.cpp-db.com

Australian Psychologists Press
142-144 Leicester Street
P.O. Box 191, Carlton South
Victoria 3053, Australia
Tel: (61) 39 349 2199
Fax: (61) 39 349 2155
E-mail: app@ozonline.com.au
Website: www.austpsychpress.com.au

Oxford Psychologists Press, Ltd.
Lambourne House
311-321 Banbury Road, Oxford
Oxon, OX2 7JH, England
Tel: (44) 1865 510203
Fax: (44) 1865 310368
E-mail: oppemail@msn.com
Website: www.opp.co.uk

Use this Form to Order *Type & Time Management*

Name: _____
      Please Print   Customer Number

Organization: _____

Address: _____
      ☐ Business   ☐ Home

City: _____

State/Province: _____ Postal Code: _____

Tel: _____ Tel: _____
   Home   Business

Fax: _____ email: _____
    ☐ Business ☐ Home   ☐ Send online newsletter (contains discounts)

Method of Payment

☐ Cheque/Money Order ☐ Visa ☐ MasterCard ☐ Purchase Order #: _____
•Please make cheques and money orders payable to Psychometrics Canada.

Card #: _____

Cardholders Name: _____ Expiry Date: ____ / ____

_____
Authorizing Signature   Date

Description	· Item #	· Qty.	· Unit Price	· Total Price
Type & Time Management	**SE01**		29.95*	

* Price is in Canadian dollars
Price in American dollars is $19.95

PSYCHOMETRICS CANADA LTD.
PSYCHOMETRICS PUBLISHING

7125 – 77 AVENUE
EDMONTON, ALBERTA
T6B 0B5, CANADA

1-800-661-5158

(780) 469-2268 Telephone (Edmonton and Area)
(780) 469-2283 Fax (area code 780 after Feb. '99)

Website: www.psychometrics.com
Email: info@psychometrics.com

Books Total	
Shipping (Ground Mail 7% of Book Sub-Total $3.00 Minimum)	
Sub-Total	
GST or HST (7% or 15% of total)	
Total Amount Due	

Photocopy as needed

Psychometrics Canada Ltd.

Enhance your abilities to use today's most advanced organizational and personal assessment tools.

For over 20 years Psychometrics Canada has been providing organizations with their choice of assessment tools, techniques and training. Effective test training techniques coupled with efficient support services are central to Psychometrics Canada's approach. Each year over 1000 HR professionals, line managers, and consultants are trained in the use of our selection, development and organization tools.

We are dedicated to:

Listening - finding out what our customers and potential customers want and how we can make them and their organizations more effective.

Innovating - combining first class research with commercial reliability to bring you products that meet your needs.

Applying - offer training courses and support materials that will help you gain immediate benefit from our products.

Those familiar with our catalogue of materials and services know that we feature the 'classics' - Myers-Briggs Type Indicator, Strong Interest Inventory, and FIRO-B which we have continuously supported and improved over the last 20 years. In addition to these we have several exciting new products which capture the latest in organizational and psychometric thinking and respond to your needs.

Call us today to find out more about Myers-Briggs Type Indicator and other qualifying workshops or for a copy of our products or workshops catalogue.
Toll Free: 1-800-661-5158